THE WICKLOW MILITARY ROAD

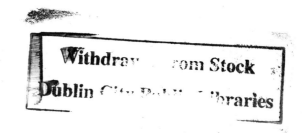

For my beautiful granddaughters, Kerry and Derbhla

THE WICKLOW Military Road

History and Topography

MICHAEL FEWER

ashfield
PRESS

Published in 2007 by
ASHFIELD PRESS • DUBLIN • IRELAND

ISBN 13: 978 1 901658 66 8

This publication has received support from the Heritage Council under the
2007 Publications Grant Scheme

This book is typeset by Ashfield Press in 11.5 on 14 point Quadraat and Frutiger
Designed by SUSAN WAINE
Printed in Ireland by BETAPRINT LIMITED, DUBLIN

Contents

By the same author

WALKS GUIDES
The Wicklow Way
Ireland's Long Distance Walks
Ireland's Way – Marked Trails
Irish Waterside Walks
Ordnance Survey Guide to the Wicklow Way
Ordnance Survey Guide to the Western Way
Ordnance Survey Guide to the Beara Way
Waterford Walks

TRAVELOGUES
By Cliff and Shore
By Swerve of Shore
Walking Across Ireland
Day Tours from Dublin

ANTHOLOGY
A Walk in Ireland

ARCHITECTURAL HISTORY
The New Neighbourhood of Dublin (with Dr. Maurice Craig)

Acknowledgements

While this is a work of history, I am not a professional historian. The last four years spent interviewing people, reading extensively about the period covered by this book, poring over dusty documents in various libraries and archives, and often taking leave of such institutions frustrated after hours of fruitless searching, leaves me only with great admiration for the supreme scholarship of the professional. My lack of professional rigor has, however, allowed me, where hard and accurate information is lacking, to make guesses that no self-respecting historian would dream of entertaining. These surmises I hope will encourage further discussion and may attract new information to accurately complete the story. Many such gaps in our knowledge about the past, where there might be an absence of good authenticating evidence, cry out for imaginative discussion to get closer to the truth, rather than leaving all the questions under a blanket of silence.

I live beside the Military Road, and as a frequent visitor to the moorlands of the Dublin and Wicklow mountains I have used it many times and grown more curious with every year that passed about its origin. One particular publication encouraged me to embark on this book: *Alexander Taylor's Roadworks in Ireland, 1780-1827* by Peter O'Keefe introduced me to this fascinating Scottish surveyor, and I have leaned heavily here on Mr. O'Keefe's scholarship and research. I was fortunate to meet many people on my journey along and through the Military Road who were happy to generously contribute stories and share their sources, photographs and contacts, and particularly enjoyed the encouragement of Jonathan Williams, Kieran Swords and my wife Teresa. The staff in The National Archives, The National Library, The Royal Society of Antiquaries, and The Irish Architectural

Archive have as always been of inestimable assistance. My particular thanks is due to South Dublin County Council and South Dublin Libraries for their assistance with the costs of my research, and I have enjoyed the help of Breda Bollard, Tom Fewer, Padraig Laffan, Kevin J. O'Connell, Kevin Lawless, Robert Butler, John McDonald, Eamon Lynch, Paddy Clarke, Tim O'Regan, Aeneas Higgins, Gloria and Paddy Smith, Tom McGuirk, Brendan Crowley, Pat Fleming, Ann and Pat Dowling, Roger White, Frank Murray, David Sheehy, Eddie McGrane, Fionan de Barra, Seamus O'Neill, Hilary O'Kelly and Fr Michael Hughes of the Oblate Fathers.

Introduction

Although not widely understood or regarded as such, roads are an important part of our built heritage. It seems certain that most of the routes we use today can be traced back many centuries, and a number of cross-country routes have their origins long before that, when man began to create permanent settlements in Ireland. The Neolithic was the first industrial and commercial age; many of the stone and flint tools of the period found in Ireland originated from the north-east, which means that the flints and axe-heads mined and prepared in County Antrim and on Rathlin Island were distributed to all parts of the country by the first commercial travellers. From that time on, cross-country routes became important arteries of our society, along which not only material goods were transported from place to place, but also the ideas that constantly advanced the thinking of society.

The Wicklow Military Road is a relatively new road in the Irish context. It is barely two hundred years in existence, and was built in time of political strife for a military purpose: the neutralisation of the Wicklow wilderness as a place of asylum for rebels and bandits. During the period of its construction, the remaining rebels finding sanctuary in the mountains dwindled away, and by the time it was completed, it had fulfilled its purpose. This publication examines the history of the road and the topography of the zone through which it passes, using it as a route to access and explore its natural history and social history. The road proceeds from Rathfarnham, County Dublin for over 60km through a rich variety of terrain, including city suburbs, woodland, moorland, an upland village and high mountain passes, to come to an end at the hamlet of Aghavannagh in County Wicklow. One could say that it proceeds through time as well as space, and in this book I have tried to weave together the threads of the road's history, landscape and built heritage.

The Origins of the Wicklow Military Road   I

The defeat of the main rebel army at Vinegar Hill in Wexford on 21 June was the beginning of the end of the 1798 Rebellion, one of the most tragic events in modern Irish history. In spite of its very short duration, a mere few weeks, the uprising had been a horrendous affair, taking the lives of more than 30,000 people, including many women and children. While the United Irishmen movement was inclusive of both Protestants and Catholics, the events that took place before, during and after the rebellion created a great chasm between Protestants and Catholics in general. Although the battle at Vinegar Hill was the last major military encounter, the spirit of the rebellion had not been entirely crushed there, and many of the rebels continued guerrilla activities, mainly in Wicklow and Kildare, during an aftermath that could be said to have lasted until the failure of Robert Emmet's uprising in Dublin in 1803.

After 21 June, however, most of the defeated rebels dispersed and made their way home, singly or in groups, some quietly and some through a series of bloody skirmishes, harried as they went by forces of local yeomanry. The nature of the fighting that had taken place during the rebellion and the atrocities that had been carried out against rural loyalists fuelled a revengeful orgy by local loyalist gentry and yeomanry. There were local scores to be settled, and the cruelties against the peasantry, which had done so much to spark the rebellion in the first place, were now carried out with renewed energy and with a more marked sectarian bias. Hangings, floggings and burnings were

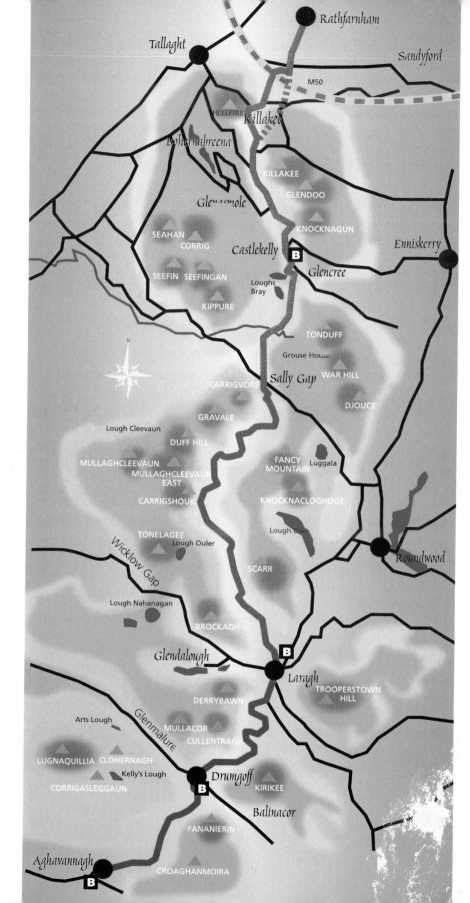

indiscriminately visited upon the Catholic peasantry on a widespread basis, some punishments directed by local magistrates, others simply the acts of revenge of local loyalists. Some sections of the army, particularly those forces under General Sir John Moore, attempted to halt the carnage and cool down the situation, while another faction under General Lake enthusiastically assisted the loyalists, carrying out awful acts of massacre and butchery.

In the midst of this chaotic maelstrom the Lord Lieutenant of Ireland, Lord Camden, was recalled to England. Since his appointment in 1795 to replace the pro-emancipation Earl of Fitzwilliam, he had shown an inability to handle the growing discontent in Ireland and had dealt poorly with the rebellion. His replacement, Charles Cornwallis, arrived in Dublin on 20 June 1798 with instructions to put matters right in Ireland, militarily and politically. A combination of career soldier and career statesman, he had already enjoyed a very active and successful international career in both spheres.

Born the son of an earl in 1738, Cornwallis entered the army at the age of eighteen, and spent the next two years attending the Military Academy in Turin. At twenty-one, he was Aide-de-camp to Lord Granby and, serving in Germany with the armies of Frederick the Great of Prussia, was present at the battle of Minden in 1759. By 1761 he had attained the rank of Lieutenant Colonel in the 12th Regiment of Foot, and was seen as an officer of considerable personal valour, who had great skill in handling his troops. On the death of his father he became the 2nd Earl Cornwallis and took his seat in the House of Lords, replacing soldiering with politics. There he earned a reputation as an active liberal, particularly on the matter of the American colonies, and in recognition of his contributions he was named Aide-de-camp to George III in 1765 and in 1770 was made Constable of the Tower of London and Vice-Treasurer of Ireland.

By 1775 he had returned to the army, promoted to the rank of Lieutenant General. He was posted to the American colonies, where it was felt the combination of his military and diplomatic talents would make a contribution. For the next six years he was closely involved in the American War of Independence, playing a significant part in decisive actions such as the Battle of New York, the Battle of Brandywine and the

Battle of Monmouth. Towards the end of 1781, in command of an army of 7,000 men, he found himself trapped at Yorktown by a force of 18,000 Americans under the command of General Washington. Expected reinforcements failing to arrive from the sea, Cornwallis reluctantly but wisely surrendered, an act which effectively brought an end to the American war.

In 1785, after a period in the wilderness, Cornwallis was appointed to the court of Frederick the Great, and the following year promoted to the rank of Field Marshal and made Governor General of India by Prime Minister Pitt. On arrival in India he applied himself to the re-organisation of the country into separate administrative districts and carried out an important series of reforms, mainly aimed at stamping out the corruption that was widespread at the time. His military background came into use again when he defeated in battle Prince Tippoo of Mysore, who had attacked and threatened adjacent states.

In 1794 he was back in England, and was appointed as the Master of Ordnance, which gave him a seat in Cabinet. At the age of sixty, and after forty-two years' service to the crown, one would have felt he would have welcomed retirement. Instead, as the 1798 rebellion wound down in Ireland, he was sent there as Lord Lieutenant and supreme commander of the army, and he was once again able to bring to bear his considerable military and political experience.

Cornwallis was a modest man: he arrived in Ireland on the ordinary packet boat, and instead of moving directly into the viceregal apartments in Dublin Castle when he arrived, he set up office instead in the humbler and less pretentious viceregal lodge in the Phoenix Park. From the beginning, his austere pattern of day-to-day governing and avoidance of lavish spending on ceremonial affairs did not enamour him with the Irish gentry. Although appointed to take up two posts, that of Lord Lieutenant and commander of the army, and entitled to take two salaries, he refused the military salary, deeming the Lord Lieutenant's salary adequate. His qualities of statesmanship allowed him to sense the mood of the populace, both the masses and the establishment, which informed his military policies. Three days after his arrival in Ireland, he wrote to a friend that 'the violence of our friends and their folly in endeavouring to make it a religious war,

Charles Cornwallis
Courtesy of the National Library of Ireland

added to the ferocity of our troops who delight in murder, most powerfully counteract all plans of conciliation'.[1]

Within days he set about efforts to calm down the situation in Wexford, Wicklow and Kilkenny, ordering General Lake in particular to practise restraint. He attempted to stamp out the indiscriminate cruelties of the yeomen and magistrates, insisting that no punishments

---

1 *Cornwallis Correspondence*, Vol II, p. 355.

or executions were to be carried out without the confirmation of an army general, which was better than what he saw as the 'numberless murders' hourly committed by loyalists 'without any process or examination whatever'.[2] Such was his commitment to the need to be seen to be acting in a more humane manner that he was prepared to personally intervene in individual cases. When it came to his notice that a Military Court Martial had acquitted a yeoman who had killed a man in the presence of witnesses in Delgany, County Wicklow, he ordered the court martial to be dismissed and the establishment of a new court to retry the case.

It was not going to be possible to capture or imprison even a small fraction of the great number of rebels who had been active during the rebellion, so the pragmatic Cornwallis instructed his generals to capture the leaders of uprising, but to offer an amnesty to all the rank and file who handed up their arms, confessed their involvement in the rebellion, took an oath of allegiance and promised to keep the peace. Those who complied were to be given a 'certificate of protection', and allowed to return to their homes. By 26 July 1798 more than 1,200 Wicklow men who had escaped from County Wexford had already surrendered their arms and received their 'certificate of protection' from the army at Blessington. The concept of the certificate of protection might have brought about a swift end to the matter if the army had been able to back it up, but in many cases the return of unarmed rebels to their homes was seen by loyalists as an opportunity to settle scores and get some satisfaction for the hardships they had endured during the rebellion. The murders, beatings and burnings that had followed in the wake of Vinegar Hill continued unabated and attended many of the homecomings, with in some cases United Irishmen being forced to eat their 'certificate' before being killed and their houses burned. In any event, the confirmation of amnesty, which constituted a pardon, had to be signed by the king, and this did not occur until October, by which time it was too late.

The army commander in Wicklow, General Moore, wrote at the time:

---

2   Letter from Cornwallis to Ross, 14 July 1798, *Cornwallis Correspondence*.

I am convinced the country would be quite [sic] if the gentlemen and yeomen could behave themselves with tolerable decency and prudence: but I am constantly obliged to reprove their violence which prompts them every instant, notwithstanding the orders and proclamations, to gratify their revenge and ill humour upon the poor inhabitants. I cannot but think that it was their harshness and ill-treatment that in great measure drove the peasants and farmers to revolt. [3]

General Moore spent some weeks in Wicklow attempting to halt the carnage, including issuing wanted notices for yeomen involved in killing men who were in receipt of certificates of protection, but the problem had by then gone too far. Faced with the chances of flogging or death on their return home, large numbers of men who had already given up their arms and received certificates fled instead into the mountains for safety and banded together. In particular, many rallied to the sides of two leaders who had taken part in the rebellion, Joseph Holt, a Protestant from near Roundwood, and Michael Dwyer, a Catholic from Glenmalure. To further complicate matters, a state of general lawlessness swept the country as gangs of disaffected rebels and military deserters, taking advantage of the chaos in the wake of the rebellion, embarked on an orgy of robbing and looting of isolated houses and settlements.

Although Joseph Holt had served as a sub-constable and had been a member of his local Volunteer corps, by the late 1790s he had become a United Irishman and his home was burned by loyalists in May 1798. There is little documentary evidence of his activities during May and early June 1798 and while it is thought he was involved in the fighting in Wexford, his own memoirs, published in a much edited form in 1838, give no details. He turned up, however, in west Wicklow in mid-June and gathered a small army at Whelp's Rock in the mountains above the town of Blessington. Here he established a makeshift camp where he shaped the dejected rebels into an effective fighting force with the intention of continuing the rebellion by waging

---

3   *The Diary of Sir John Moore*, edited by J. F. Maurice, 1904.

guerrilla war on the loyalists until the expected French invasion. On 25 June Holt led his men on a successful attack on the little town of Hackettstown in east Carlow, and a couple of days later achieved a significant military victory against a mounted force of yeomanry, leaving fifty of them for dead. During a disastrous foray into County Meath, however, in the hope of stirring up popular support there, Holt suffered a series of defeats, during one of which he was left for dead. Returning to the safety of the mountains he continued his personal war for the next couple of months with ambushes of yeomanry troops and attacks on loyalist settlements: 400 properties were put to the torch by his band.[4] It is clear from contemporary accounts that Holt's little army was a disciplined force, and his men were strongly discouraged from looting and robbing.

A day after the ending of the long-awaited French invasion with the defeat of General Humbert in September 1798, Joseph Holt decided there was little point in persevering in his struggle, and he set about seeking the most favourable terms for his surrender. He spent the next couple of months making approaches to the authorities, initially through the influential La Touche family, by whom he felt he would be sympathetically treated: his wife's family had been tenants of theirs and was known to them, and Holt had on one occasion personally prevented his men from torching David La Touche's hunting lodge at Luggala. Through these connections he negotiated his surrender to Lord Powerscourt and gave himself up on 10 November 1798. He had agreed to be transported to Van Diemen's Land with his family and this eventually took place, but he was allowed to return to Ireland in 1814, where he became the proprietor of an inn at Cuffe Street, and wrote his memoirs of the rebellion. He died in 1826 and is buried in Monkstown, County Dublin.

Michael Dwyer was a small farmer from south Wicklow. He joined the United Irishmen in 1797 and was quickly recognised to have excellent leadership qualities. He was involved in the Battle of Arklow and subsequently Vinegar Hill, before escaping back to the Wicklow Mountains and, like Holt, attracted a gathering of rebels keen to

---

4   *General Holt*, Ruan O'Donnell pp. 170-171, 179.

continue the fight. From his hideout in the mountains, his little army carried out sporadic raids on settlements and villages and 'kept the county in perpetual alarms'. The postmaster of Rathdrum wrote to the Secretary of the Post Office in October 1798:

> ...they came to within 1 mile of this town and burned all respectable Houses for a mile and a half betwixt this and the mountains – commanded by one Dwire one of General Moore's pets – who along with some more of our generals contributed to the ruin of this once happy country....[5]

One of the main reasons for the survival in Wicklow of Holt's forces until November 1798 and Dwyer's until December 1803 was the relative inaccessibility of the central Wicklow mountain area, where they established a number of safe hideouts.

It is generally accepted that, by the end of the 18th century, the quality of the roads in general in Ireland was superior to those in England. This superiority can be attributed in the main to two pieces of legislation. Firstly, the awarding in 1739 of compulsory purchase powers to landlord-controlled Grand Juries for the purpose of providing public roads, allowing roads to be locally controlled and financed from local taxes, and secondly, the abolition in Ireland in 1763 of the antiquated system of unpaid Statute Labour, which remained in force much longer in England.[6] The success of this local method of providing roads in Ireland is born out by the fact that it was not until the very end of the 18th century that the State needed to become involved in the provision of roads: the first such road was the military road from Waterford to Cork, completed in 1789.

While the road network we use today in Ireland was, therefore, all but established by the end of the 18th century, there remained a few

---

5 *The Life of Michael Dwyer*, Charles Dickson, p. 51.
6 Statute Labour came into force in 1555 with the first Highway Act, which put the responsibility for maintaining the roads on the parishes within whose boundaries they ran, requiring inhabitants of each parish to give six days per year unpaid labour towards the work. The unpopular and unsuccessful system was to continue in England until the end of the 18th century.

areas where the influence of the roads engineers had not extended, notably west Kerry, west Mayo and central Wicklow. An extensive area of mountains and high moorland in Wicklow was inaccessible, but for three east/west routes: an ancient pathway over the Sally Gap between Blessington and Togher (Roundwood), a somewhat better one over the Wicklow Gap between Hollywood and Laragh, and another partial track up the Valley of Glenmalure and over the top of Table Mountain, connecting Rathdrum with Donard. These routes were unsuitable for all but rugged pedestrians and equestrians, and then only during periods of dry weather. The only north to south roads of any worth close to the uplands were the road from Enniskerry to Togher and on to Laragh and Rathdrum on the east, and the road from Dublin to Blessington and on to Donard and Hackettstown on the west. This left a tract of land of over 300 square miles, much of which was inhospitable high moorland, but with valleys that secreted plenty of sheltered, secluded areas where a winter could be endured with ease. It was in these sanctuaries that the Wicklow wilderness provided a refuge for the followers of Holt and Dwyer, inaccessible to all but small, lightly armed detachments of military, and then only if they could exercise the element of surprise.

When not engaged in marauding activities, the rebels tended to disperse into small groups of three or four for convenience of accommodation and access to food. The rural people in Wicklow willingly took them into their homes, and there are many records even of local yeomen providing food and shelter on a frequent basis.

The successful pursuit of raiding parties across mountain moorland by the military was extremely difficult; when on the move, the rebels needed to carry no provisions since they could depend on the peasantry for food, they had no problems abandoning or hiding their arms, and travelling very lightly in this way with local knowledge or guides, they were able to disperse and merge swiftly into the general mountain populace. Frequent sweeps were carried out into the mountains by the military and the yeomanry in the hope of catching the rebels, and especially their leaders, with little success. Indeed, most of the legendary stories about Dwyer in particular deal with his many near miraculous escapes from capture rather than his marauding activities.

Although visual telegraphic signalling was well developed at the time and practised by the military, such signalling was difficult in mountainous areas, and the nature of the boggy terrain of the high moors prevented the use of fast dispatch riders to take messages to other detachments in the east, west or south who might be positioned to intercept a rebel movement before they dispersed and merged with the peasantry.

While the army was attempting to deal with this situation in Wicklow, an event of a far more serious nature was unfolding on the north-west coast of Ireland, when an expeditionary force of the French Army landed in County Mayo on 22 August.

It is difficult at this remove to appreciate the enormity of the enmity that existed at the time between Britain and France. They had been at war, on and off, for years, in a mutual effort to destroy each other, and the threat of a French invasion of Ireland, the back door to Britain, was always there. By 1798, with Napoleon's armies concentrated at Boulogne threatening invasion, Britain stood alone without allies, and the position was desperate. Now, what had been most feared by the authorities in Dublin had come to pass: a significant French force under General Humbert had landed and occupied a part of County Mayo, and the Republic of Connaught had been proclaimed. In spite of being far too late to assist the rebellion and to substantially augment their forces with rebel Irish, the invasion caught the authorities by surprise and it took three weeks and much military superiority to bring the venture to an end. Cornwallis had succeeded in considerably reinforcing the army in Ireland, and although he felt that the military threat posed by the French would not be a problem, he was concerned that the presence of the French force might encourage a country-wide rebellion. He therefore took the field personally against the French, becoming the first Lord Lieutenant in a century to lead an army against an enemy, and using greatly superior forces, brought about a swift surrender by Humbert. Although a failure, this brief invasion indicated how easy it might be for a substantial French force, with rebel allies, to gain a foothold in Ireland, and thus threaten not only the Irish loyalists, but also Britain itself.

As rumblings of the rebellion continued through the autumn and into the winter of 1798, the poor harvests of the previous autumn raised the cost of food and led to additional discontent among the populace. This discontent manifested itself in general lawlessness in many parts of the country, including places that had not been involved in the fighting during the summer. In this unstable atmosphere, and with the memories of the horrors of the rebellion fresh in everyone's minds, it was not difficult to believe that the threat of yet another French invasion was sowing the seeds for fresh uprising.

The Petition for a Military Road in Wicklow 2

T he general undercurrent of discontent continued on through the following year, particularly in Wicklow, where Michael Dwyer kept up his marauding activities. The proprietors and landowners of Wicklow were extremely concerned at the increasing lawlessness emanating from the mountains and wide consideration was given to measures that would help to bring an end, finally, to the use of the mountains for refuge, which was not just a phenomenon of the late 18th century. Charles Cornwallis himself had, in fact, been giving serious consideration to the construction of a military road through the mountains that would allow army units more mobility in actions against the rebels, and in the summer of 1799 he ordered preliminary survey work to be carried out to see if it would be possible to build such a road and how much it would cost.

Much consideration had been given to building a road into the mountains during the Elizabethan period, when, in the last decades of the 16th century, Fiach MacHugh O'Byrne was such a thorn in the side of the English administration. After a number of failed attempts to penetrate the mountains from the north in an effort to get at O'Byrne's stronghold at Ballincor in the eastern end of Glenmalure, Lord Winton de Grey tried a new route in the summer of 1580 by approaching from the west with a substantial army. The venture ended in the defeat and rout of his force, and it was to be another two hundred years before the English would try to enter the uplands in any force again.

The use of military roads in Scotland in the early 18th century to open up the Highlands had been successful, and it seemed clear that a new fortified road right through the centre of Wicklow would similarly assist government forces to fully pacify the county. The results of the preliminary survey for the construction of a road were favourable, but it may be that Cornwallis did not want to be seen to be imposing such a road on the county, because it seems that he arranged that the landowners of Wicklow would petition him for it. In February 1800, therefore, a formal request for such a road was placed before Cornwallis by all the principal landowners and magistrates of County Wicklow, including the Earl of Wicklow, Lord Powerscourt and General Lord Rossmore.[7] The petition, with the title *Reason for making the new Military Road in the County of Wicklow submitted to His Excellency Major Cornwallis by the Royal Proprietors of that County, Feb. 1800*, began with the dire warning:

> As there are now evident symptoms of new disturbances in many parts of the Kingdom which will most assuredly take place should the French affect a landing or perhaps sooner, the situation of the Mountains of Wicklow demands the serious attention of the Government... .

He mentioned that in July 1798, due to the lack of connections between the existing east-west routes, four 'large armies' sent into the mountains to apprehend the 'great bodies of rebels' who were enjoying safe retreat there, found not even one rebel.

To reinforce their request, they put forward two additional scenarios, which a new road would assist in addressing. Firstly, it was suggested that if the 31,000 rebels involved in the attack on Arklow had instead assembled in the mountains and made a 'bold push' for Dublin – there were no more than 1,300 troops available at the time to

---

7   *Reason for making the new Military Road in the County of Wicklow submitted to His Excellency Major Cornwallis by the Royal Proprietors of that County, Feb. 1800*. The document (NA ref OP 293/) seems to be a transcribed copy of the original petition, because it does not have the signatures of all the petitioners, only mentioning the Earl of Wicklow, Lord Powerscourt, General Lord Rossmore 'and all the principal magistrates and gentlemen of the county Wicklow'.

defend the city – the result would have been disastrous, particularly if there had been a simultaneous rising in the city. It was felt that the rebels had learned from the mistakes they made during the late rebellion, and that there was every reason to believe that if there were another rising, it would take place in or near Dublin, and that the Wicklow mountains would provide a secure and secret gathering point for their greatest force. The second scenario skilfully sketched by the petitioners was the need to improve communications in the Wicklow area because of the belligerent French, the all-purpose bogymen of the period, and the possibility that they would attempt another landing on Irish soil to back up such a new rebellion.

The proposals outlined in the petition from the landowners had already been thoroughly discussed and agreed with all the main movers in the project, principally the landowners who would be directly affected, i.e. those through whose land the road would pass. At the time, up to 30,000 acres of the central Wicklow area, where the road would have to pass, were owned by six individual landowners. The military, it must be supposed, after centuries of frustration, were very much in favour of obtaining the means to finally establish their rule in Wicklow. Cornwallis had been appointed on 21 June 1798 not only as Lord Lieutenant but also as Commander-in-Chief of the army, and the petition allowed him to deal with the necessity for the road as a military matter.

The Martial Law Act passed in February 1799 facilitated the kind of radical action required to deal with the landowners' petition as a matter of urgency. It simply would not have been possible to make the decision to proceed with such a road, and indeed to have work begin, without such far-reaching powers, and the speed with which matters moved after the presentation of the February petition, a speed which makes contemporary 'fast-tracking' seem snail-like, would not have been possible without Cornwallis's decisiveness.

Cornwallis was a firm and committed believer in union with Britain, and in parallel with his battle to finally bring the rebellion to an end, he worked tirelessly from the moment he arrived in Ireland to lay the groundwork for union. He did not feel the general populace would have a problem with the union, commenting that 'the mass of the people of Ireland do not care one farthing about the union...' and that they 'equally hate both government and opposition' in the Irish parliament. All evidence points to the fact that he read the situation well; the Union meant little to the majority of the Irish, who had little reason or evidence to allow them to believe that London laws would be any different from the laws of the Dublin Pale. Indeed some felt that, in spite of the new liberal policies being expounded by the Irish Parliament, it had been the same parliament that had voted in the penal laws, and it was only the influence of the British Parliament that mitigated their execution. While he might have underestimated the practical difficulties that might arise, Cornwallis believed that Catholic Emancipation should be incorporated into the Union, and felt that loyalist country gentlemen had been sufficiently frightened by the rebellion to see the need to make such 'sacrifices'. The vacillating landlords and middle and upper classes needed, however, to be encouraged towards union, and he saw that the 1798 Rebellion and the ensuing unrest in the country was certainly to his advantage in this regard. The general unrest among the people also helped to secure the important support of the Catholic Hierarchy, thus further weakening the opposition. To underpin the move towards union, however, he knew it was necessary to show that London had the power to establish complete military control over rebellious sections of the population. Wicklow was, and had always been, a thorn in the establishment's side, and he saw that a military road fortified with barracks could be one of the keys to resolving the problem for once and for all.

The first documented military roads were the work of the Romans and were a vital factor in their imperial system; a network of well-designed and maintained roads was essential to provide a rapid means of trade and communications, and to assist a comparatively small military force subdue and hold a large area of territory. In Britain alone there were 5,000 miles of Roman roads, built over the four hundred years of Roman rule, and for the most part they went as straight as possible across the landscape, following the shortest and most direct route to allow the quick passage of armies through every part of the country. This was possible because the rights of civilian landowners could be ignored. The technical design of the Roman roads was very advanced for the time, and ensured they would last, as they have, for many centuries. They were generally built on a foundation of compacted earth, covered by a layer of large stones and mortar, on top of which a course of small stones bound with mortar was laid. The roads were finished by a course of lime or chalk, into which the surface of cobbles was bedded. In mainland Europe such construction has remained relatively intact in places for more than 2,000 years.

By the time the Romans had reached Britain, they had developed and refined their engineering skills to a high point of perfection, to such an extent that the quality of their roads was not really equalled until the early 18th century, when General George Wade (1673-1748) embarked upon his strategic road-building works in Scotland in the aftermath of the Jacobite Rising of 1715. Politically and physically, Scotland of the early 18th century had many similarities with the Wicklow of nearly a century later, although the Wicklow highlands were of a much smaller scale. The Scottish road network was poor at the time and in places non-existent, particularly in the Highlands, which were inhabited in the main by Scots loyal to the House of Stuart who had always posed a threat to England. In order to offset the threat of revolts being hatched against the English Crown, and gaining strength out of sight of the authorities, it was decided to open up the Highlands by the construction of a number of strategic roads and the placing of garrisons throughout the region.

General Wade was born in County Westmeath and, entering the army in 1690, distinguished himself over the next three decades in military actions in France, Spain and Portugal. In 1726 he was appointed commander-in-chief of the army in the Highlands of Scotland and commenced the construction of some 1,500 miles of roads and forty stone bridges. They were designed to carry heavy equipment, including artillery, and were built almost entirely by soldiers, who received extra pay for their work. Although intended for military strategic reasons, after the Highlands became 'pacified' the new road system came into general use. Travelling and transport were so much easier on these new roads that they highlighted how bad the original road system had been throughout Scotland, and they stimulated moves towards a general improvement in road construction.

Subsequent to his arrival in Ireland in June 1798, Charles Cornwallis would have had cause on occasions to consult with General Charles Vallencey (1725-1812), Director of Engineering of the army, regarding matters of land survey maps and intelligence on areas where military action against the rebels was under consideration. It is probable that it was during the course of these consultations that Cornwallis met Vallencey's deputy, Captain Alexander Taylor, who, having surveyed and produced ordnance maps relating to that part of County Kildare which adjoins Wicklow County, would have been familiar with the Wicklow Mountain area. There was another connection between Cornwallis and Taylor: Alexander's brother, George, had applied for a post under Cornwallis in America some years before, during the War of Independence. He had commented at the time: 'it makes a difference in my pay of a dollar a day only, but puts me immediately under the eye of Lord Cornwallis, from whose good sense I expect some advantage.' He was successful in obtaining the position and not only did he gain the advantage he expected, but no doubt his brother, a couple of decades later, gained some also.

Alexander Taylor was born in Scotland in 1746; his father was William Taylor, a military surveyor based at Fort George near Inverness. Alexander did not have a formal qualification in engineering or surveying, but became a surveyor through 'serving his time' at practical surveying with a number of employers, which would have been a normal route towards becoming a professional surveyor at the time. Much of his early work was in the employment of the Duke of Gordon, where he gained much experience of survey work on the high moors and bogs of the Highlands, accurately identifying and mapping boundaries between estates and properties.

In the last quarter of the 18th century Ireland experienced an unprecedented golden age of prosperity and optimism, partly the result of nearly a century of relative domestic peace and the establishment of an Irish Parliament. With the growth of Irish cities, particularly Dublin, came a growth in communications, but there was a lack of up-to-date and reliable topographical information. Dr Peter Twiss, author in 1775 of *A Tour in Ireland*, complained that maps were 'in general erroneous, and badly executed ... merely copies of old maps'.

In most cases, the small scale of the maps available, together with the inaccuracies that will inevitably be created by time, was recognised by Grand Juries of the more prosperous counties, and led to funds being made available to grant-aid comprehensive new surveys. It was into this opportune situation that Alexander Taylor's brother, George, together with his partner, Andrew Skinner, arrived in Dublin in 1776. They had surveyed and produced *The Survey and Maps of the Roads of North Britain, or Scotland*, and had come to Ireland to propose to the country's landowners that a new survey and map of the roads of Ireland would be useful and beneficial to all.

The positive reaction they received, which apart from the support of private individuals included subscriptions from governmental agencies such as the Revenue Commissioners and the Barrack Board, encouraged them to set up office in Dublin in 1777 and commence work on *Maps of the Roads of Ireland*.

During that year Taylor and Skinner employed two surveyors and sixteen other men in surveying 8,000 miles of road, and it is possible that Alexander Taylor came over from Scotland for the duration of the project as one of the two surveyors.[8] After this first visit to Ireland, Alexander Taylor returned to Scotland and in December 1777 joined the 81st Regiment of Foot regiment as a military surveyor with the rank of lieutenant. He was back again the following year when the regiment was transferred to Ireland.

In 1779 Taylor began to work on a part-time basis with Lieutenant Colonel Charles Vallencey, then Director of Engineering of the army, carrying out surveying work for what had been planned as a comprehensive military survey of Ireland but which was only eventually completed for the south-east of the country. The work had commenced in 1776, and it took twenty years to complete the stretch from 40 miles south of Dublin as far as Cork Harbour. During the course of the work, Taylor became indispensable to Vallencey, and the nature of his involvement on the Military Survey allowed him also to carry on some 'private' work, which included the 1783 Map of the County of Kildare,

---

8   Paper by J. H. Andrews in Kildare Archaeological Society Journal, Vol. 16, pp. 89-96 (1977).

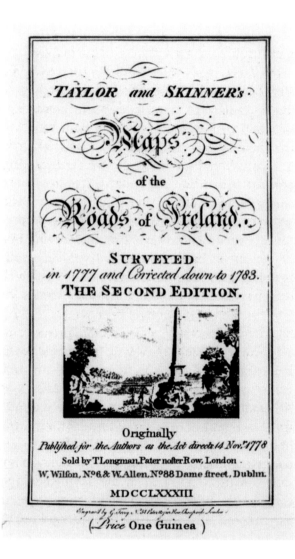

Front plate of Taylor & Skinner's *Maps of the Roads of Ireland.*

which shows considerable detail in roads, hills, rivers, bogs, antiquities and slated farmhouses etc., and carrying out the revisions to the second edition of the *Maps of the Roads of Ireland.* He spent some months, possibly as many as five, in Paris with Vallencey in 1787 copying the 214 original maps from the Petty Survey, which had been captured by the French in 1707, and it is to be supposed that the two men would have got to know each other very well during this sojourn.

Vallencey was a man of many parts and many interests. In his spare time he was a member of the Royal Irish Academy and the Dublin Society, and was a very interested, interesting but often inaccurate commentator on a wide range of matters from ogham writing to the Irish language. As he got older, he devoted more and more of his time to these cultural activities, and although making sure he was properly paid for all his efforts on behalf of the crown, seems to have eventually delegated many of his surveying projects to Taylor. Certainly by 1787 it seems that he had become Vallencey's deputy and was supervising most of the real survey work on the ground. By the end of the century Taylor must have developed a solid reputation as a surveyor, mapmaker and engineer in his own right, and having spent his early career as a surveyor in the Scottish Highlands, he would have been not only familiar with surveying moors and mountains, but would also have been acquainted with General Wade's Military Roads.

Within a week or two of his receipt of the petition from the landowners of Wicklow, Lord Cornwallis issued, through his Military Under Secretary, E. B. Littlehales, an official instruction to General Vallencey that a survey be carried out and a cost estimate be prepared for the construction of a military road through Wicklow. The orders specified that Captain Alexander Taylor of the Engineers should be the surveyor in charge of the project. No mention is made in the documentation at this stage that in the summer of 1799 Taylor had already carried out, at the Lord Lieutenant's request, a preliminary survey of the terrain the road would have to be built through, and probably planned, in outline, the route.

Poor weather conditions in Wicklow in the spring of 1800 prevented Taylor from starting his detailed field survey for the road until early in April, but it is likely that considerable preparatory work was done while he waited for the weather to improve, using Jacob Neville's 1760 map of County Wicklow and the revised version prepared by the latter's nephew Arthur Neville in 1798, combined with the data Taylor had collected the previous year.

The lie of the land in the central Wicklow range is not difficult to ascertain: initial work would have been confined to selecting the most appropriate north/south passes between the hills to use, and after that, relatively simple levelling work would have identified the best contours to follow to connect the passes. All the summits along the route, and most of the route itself, were devoid of trees, and in clear weather with good telescopic equipment, which we assume Taylor must have had available to him, sightings and levels would have been easy to take in good visibility.

He had, after all, had a preliminary look at the terrain for a road in 1799, and it seems that he took little time to identify and confirm the best route across the mountains, and early in the survey had chosen Rathfarnham as a starting point.

The purpose of the Military Road, apart from the improvement of military communications throughout Wicklow and the placing of a chain of permanent garrisons down through the centre of the county, was to allow the deployment of large army forces and all their supplies, from their barracks in Dublin into the mountains at speed or from any part of Wicklow to another part.

In 1800, three main roads issued towards the mountains from the southern suburbs of Dublin city, the limits of which did not extend far beyond Harcourt Street,[9] well inside the Grand Canal. The most westerly road was the main road to Tallaght, by Dolphin's Barn, via Crumlin. The most easterly road was at the time the main road to Milltown and Dundrum, via Rathmines or Ranelagh, and issued from the city by Charlotte Street, an extension to Camden Street. The middle road was the main road to Rathfarnham, by New Street, an extension of Patrick's Street, and Harold's Cross. The central mountain area, the optimum line for an effective military road, would have been accessible from Tallaght via Bohernabreena and Glenasmole, or from Dundrum via Kilgobbin and Glencullen, but the shortest and most direct route into the mountains, even if the most challenging, was clearly from Rathfarnham. Rathfarnham was also ideally placed in relation to its communications with Dublin, to which it was connected by a good, straight modern road. The line of this road is said to be that

---

9   Survey of Dublin for the use of the Divisional Justices, 1797 (see *Malton's Dublin* 1799, Dolmen Press 1978).

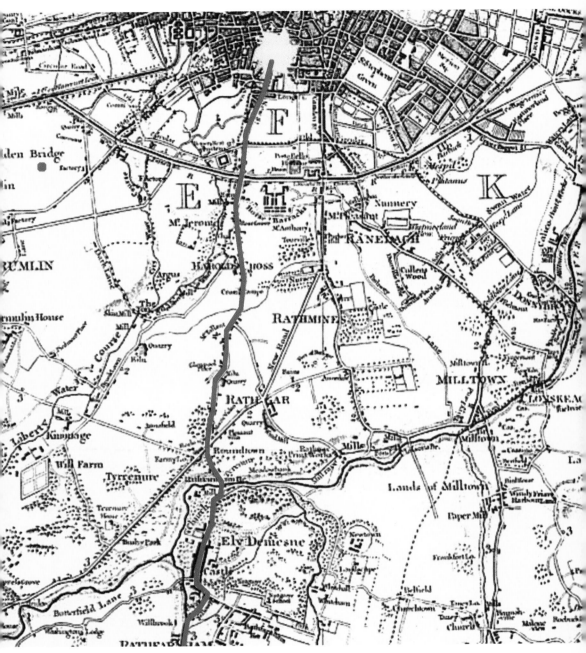

John Taylor's Map of 1816. The route from the city to Rathfarnham is marked in red, and the Military Road is marked in green

of one of the Five Great Roads, the ancient Slighe Chualann, which ran from Waterford through Dublin to Tara, meeting the Slighe Dhala at the Coombe. The only physical interruption along the route between central Dublin and Rathfarnham was the Dodder River, which was bridged in 1765. It was a substantial single arch bridge and, widened in 1953, it still serves. Previous to the 1765 bridge, a number of timber structures spanned the river here, the earliest dating from about 1381: there are records that state that a Joan Douce, of St Audoen's parish in Dublin, contributed the sum of one mark towards its construction.[10] Evidence that this was a busy and important crossing point even long before this, however, was found when, in 1912, during the excavations for a drainage scheme, a nine-foot-wide causeway or ford, built of great slabs of stone, was found crossing the course of the river. The stones bore the parallel grooves from many years of the passage of wheeled traffic.

Using this middle route in 1800, it is clear that an army of foot soldiers, cavalry and artillery would have little difficulty travelling quickly from the centre of the city as far south as Rathfarnham. Indeed, there was at the time a vast cavalry barracks at Portobello, stretching from the route at Harold's Cross Road eastwards to Rathmines Road. Rathfarnham, therefore, being close to the mountains and with good communications with the city, was recommended by Taylor as the starting point for the Military Road.

From the southern end of Rathfarnham village in 1800 the road known today as Willbrook Road ran southwards into the foothills. While neither Rocques' 1760 map of County Dublin, nor Frizell's 1779 map of Rathfarnham shows Willbrook Road, it is shown on John Byrne's 1801 map of Rathfarnham and is indicated on a sketch map drawn by Alexander Taylor c.1804 as a road that pre-existed the new Military Road.

The Owendoher and Whitechurch, fast-flowing mountain streams descending from the foothills towards the Dodder, were of ideal size and flow for the development of watermills. Between the early 18th century and the arrival of economic industrial steampower in the early

10 Balls *History of the County Dublin*, Vol. II, p.116.

Rathfarnham Bridge: at the far side the 1953 extension is clearly visible

19th century watermills proliferated along these streams, and the area became one of the earliest places in County Dublin to become industrialised. There had been a papermill in Rathfarnham since 1719, and in 1800, between the village and Rockbrook, 4km to the south, there were two corn mills, eight paper mills, and one flour mill strung along the Owendoher River alone. There was also a corn mill at Kilmashogue and a threshing mill at Marlay. The mills along the Owendoher would have needed a good and direct road connecting them with Rathfarnham and Dublin, and it seems likely that the road we know today as Willbrook Road, and its extension up along the east

bank of the Owendoher as far Billy's Bridge where it met a pre-existing road leading on to Rockbrook, was built some time between 1779 and 1800.

Making use of his considerable experience of moorland work in Scotland and his earlier reconnaissance, Taylor was able to complete the surveying of the proposed route for the Military Road within a month, and his report and an estimate of cost for the road were submitted to the Lord Lieutenant's office by early May. Again Cornwallis did not delay, and within a week of receiving Taylor's report he had ordered the work of constructing the road to proceed – a letter dated 15 May 1800 to Lord Rossmore, one of the signatories of the Proprietor's Memorandum, states that 'Captain Taylor has secured my Lord Lieutenant's commands to begin the Mountain Road early in the ensuing month'.

Simultaneous with Taylor's preparations for the construction of the road, other moves were afoot to take control of the existing mountain roads in Wicklow, on which few felt they could travel without fear of attack by bandits since the autumn of 1798. *The Freeman's Journal* in June 1800 carried the following proclamation by Lieutenant Colonel George Stewart, designed to assure the loyal citizens of Wicklow that the army was now in control of the area:

> Notice is hearby given that the Mountain roads are now opened by the troops under my Command, and the following places are now occupied by them, viz, The Glen of Imail, the Lugnaquilla Mountain, the Glen Maher (Malure), Balnabarny Gap, the Roads to it, the Aughavannagh Road, the Roads at and near Ballymanus, Aughrim, Ballynaclash, Rathdrum, and the Roads on the River Avon to the Seven Churches and all the Mountains near them, Annamoe, Roundwood, the Wicklow Gap Road and Mountains, Hollywood, Glenbride, Knocknadruce, the Mountain Roads to Blessington, the Hill of Adown, all the Luggalaw Road, and to the Douce Mountain and the Mountains of Rathfarnham.

John Byrne's Map of the south of Rathfarnham in 1801. The Military Road is highlighted in red. Note the Yellow House at the beginning of ◄— the road. Courtesy of Roger White

The possession of these Roads, Passes and Mountains will most effectually open the Country, and enable me to protect the persons and the property of all its loyal inhabitants, in and near them and to protect them when carrying the produce of the Country to the Markets of the Towns below, and will afford them an opportunity of destroying the Banditti that now infest the County; it will also enable the people to travel with safety to the Mountains at all times, and to bring provisions to His Majesty's Troops there, who will pay the Market price for it; and I will give immediate protection to any of the inhabitants who shall assist me, or any detachment of the troops, in securing any of the gang of Robbers headed by Michael Dwyer.

Given under my hand at Camp on Lugnaquilla Mountain, the 19th day of June, 1800.

Stewart's efforts came to little, however, as did the next serious military attempt to finish off the rebels, carried out by the Somerset Fencibles under Major Tattam in December 1801. Reinforced by the Duke of York's Highlanders and parties of local yeomanry, Tattam closed in on Aghavannagh where intelligence said the Dwyer's men were meeting. Word was passed swiftly, however, to Dwyer, and by the time the military got into Aghavannagh, the rebels had faded away.

There is no evidence of any legal acquisitions being carried out of the land over which the Military Road would pass: most of the larger landowners involved, such as the owners of the Powerscourt, Beresford, Hugo, Bishopsland, Meath, Kemmis and Cutwell estates,[11] were not only signatories of the petition to have a road built, but content to give up the land required, confident that the road would put an end to their problems with Dwyer and that such development in their hitherto inaccessible lands might soon be followed by settlement, trade and increased rents.

To begin the work on the road, Taylor requested and received approval from Cornwallis to employ two hundred infantry soldiers of the Fencible and Militia Corps on the work, and they were to be paid an extra shilling over and above their normal day's pay for the work

---

11 William Nolan (ed.), *Wicklow History and Society* Chapter 16.

carried out on the project. Fencible regiments were made up of full-time regular soldiers: they were initially raised in wartime for the defence of their homeland and were limited to this homeland service unless all the members of a regiment voted to go overseas. Between 1793 and 1802 about fifteen Scottish Fencible infantry regiments and one Fencible cavalry regiment, the Royal Edinburgh Light Dragoons, served in Ireland, and many, such as the Dumbartonshire Fencibles, who fought in the Battle of Arklow, saw action during the rebellion.[12] As the country returned to normality after the rebellion, disbandment of the Fencible regiments began, and it is possible that the men who went to work for Taylor saw the opportunity of prolonging their paid service by volunteering for the work on the road. At one shilling a day extra to their normal pay, seven shillings a week, it was a good job to have. Sergeants were paid one shilling and sixpence extra, and three subalterns at a rate of five shillings each a day were also placed under Taylor's command. Approval to advance funds to the project was given on 10 August 1800 when Cornwallis approved the 'immediate' release of the first £100, to be followed by a sum of £1,000, to Lieutenant Ginkel, who had been appointed as the Paymaster for the project at a rate of seven shillings and sixpence per day.[13]

Taylor requisitioned and received two hundred spades, two hundred shovels, thirty pickaxes, forty handbarrows and twenty crowbars to begin the work. The normal equipment of an army regiment would have included much of the other hardware required, i.e. wagons, hoists, tents, etc., as well as horses. He was also given permission and promised funding to employ up to two hundred local people on the works.

---

12 T. F. Mills, Fencible Regiments of the British Army.
13 Letter from E.B. Littlehales, 10 August 1800 (Kilmainham Papers).

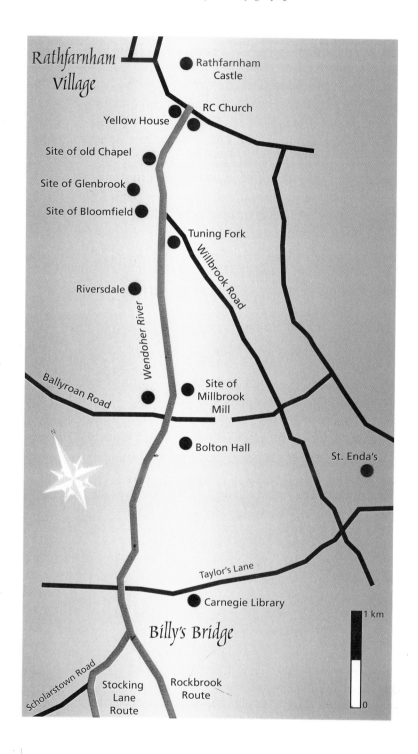

The Military Road from Rathfarnham Village to Billy's Bridge

Work on the road began in August 1800, a mere eight months after the petition for such had been received by Charles Cornwallis; such speed of execution was only made possible because the military, in the aftermath of the rebellion, had the manpower, the resources and an element of martial freedom to override any normal peacetime or legal hitches that might otherwise arise in the matter. In the initial stages it is clear from the documentation available that the project was regarded as a major priority; E. B. Littlehales, the military under-secretary to the Lord Lieutenant, refers repeatedly in correspondence related to the project to those who work on 'this special service'.

Although the route known today as the Wicklow Military Road runs from the village of Rathfarnham into the Dublin and Wicklow mountains as far as the hamlet of Aghavannagh, some sections of the road were already in existence when Taylor began work in August 1800, and may have required, at most, some repairs. The longest such stretch was the 6½ statute mile roadway between Rathfarnham and the hamlet of Rockbrook.

From Rockbrook, Taylor planned to cut through the lands of Killakee to reach the open mountainside.

A considerable amount of preparatory work had to be carried out and completed before construction work could begin, not least of which was the provision of living quarters and arrangements for providing food and bedding for the two hundred men who would carry out the work. Taylor seems to have considered that the location and type of living quarters provided was critical to the success of the venture. An encampment of tents would in other circumstances have been the ideal way of dealing with the problem: as the road extended, the tent camp would be struck regularly and moved forward with the road, so the distance to and from the work would be kept to a minimum. Weather conditions in the mountains, however, would have made living in tents hard in other than fine summer weather, and we know that Taylor had already experienced how winter conditions can be prolonged in the mountains when he was forced in early 1800 to delay his survey work until April. The urgency of the need for the provision of the road was such that Taylor knew work could not be limited solely to summer months.

There is a folk memory in the Ballyboden neighbourhood south of Rathfarnham that some of the Fencible soldiers were 'boarded out' in the old village there during the initial stages of the project. While this would have been a common procedure for armies at the time, it is unlikely that more than a few men, probably based there to 'upgrade' the existing road, would have been billeted in the village for any length of time. Apart from the logistics of getting enough billets for bedding and feeding for two hundred men, beyond Ballyboden there would have been few opportunities to make use of local billets: apart from a small number of cottiers living at the head of Glencree valley at a place called Aurora,[14] the high moorland was uninhabited almost as far as Laragh.

Another factor would have influenced Taylor's decision regarding living quarters for his men. Viscount Powerscourt, who had been one of the signatories of the petition to Cornwallis for a military road, managed to use his influence to persuade the authorities that a spur connection from the road to his estate village of Enniskerry would be advisable. Taylor was ordered to build this spur, probably on the basis that it would give direct access to the Wicklow coast from the Military Road, and anyway such a road would have been useful as a supply route in the early stages of road construction.

---

14 The origin of Aurora, the Latin for dawn, is unknown but, according to Liam Price, first mention of it appears in the Powerscourt Estate records of 1757.

When the work of constructing the Military Road commenced in August 1800, Taylor established a headquarters or main base near Aurora in Glencree, 12 miles from Rathfarnham and 6 miles from Enniskerry. With the permission of the landowner, Lord Powerscourt, he started his men constructing a work camp of huts south-east of where Glencree Barracks was subsequently built. There is no trace of this encampment two hundred years later, but the 'Soldiers' Huts' must have been substantial, as we know the materials for their construction cost £230.[15] There is a field near the little settlement of Aurora called the Camp, surrounded by a substantial stone wall, which is thought to be the site of the hut village, and another field nearby is still called the Hospital Field, a name, it is said, that also dates back to the time of the Fencible encampment. Less than a mile from the camp at Glencree, above the two Loughs Bray, there is a high granite promontory called Eagles Crag, which, with an uninterrupted view of the route of the road for nearly 10km from the Featherbeds on down to near the Sally Gap, made an excellent survey station. On the flat granite slab that forms the top of the crag are a series of 25mm drilled holes, which were probably put there by Taylor or his assistants to take the theodolite tripod.

From the encampment of huts in Glencree it seems that Taylor began work on the road construction simultaneously on three separate sections: from Glencree to Rathfarnham, from Glencree southwards towards the Sally Gap and Laragh, and from Glencree to Enniskerry. Each section would have been under the command of one of the three subalterns who had been assigned to him. In the early stages of construction, supplies for the soldiers would have been brought to Glencree by way of bridal paths from Enniskerry or from Tallaght via Glenasmole or from Rathfarnham. The raw materials for the road, consisting at this stage mainly of granite rocks and gravel, were plentiful under the covering of peat, and numerous small quarries can be seen today along the route of the road from where the soldiers took stone. The only interruptions would have been where the road had to bridge streams, where bridge structures that required large slabs of good granite were needed. A good road was needed to transport such loads,

---

15   Taylor's Report of 10 February 1802 NA Official Papers 293/1(11).

and it is possible that these crossings were left in abeyance initially, until the road was extended to where suitable granite could be brought in.

The beginning of the Wicklow Military Road, called Willbrook Road today, can be found at the southern end of Rathfarnham Village, heading south for the mountains from Rathfarnham Road, flanked by the Yellow House pub and the Roman Catholic Church.

The Yellow House is a late 19th-century building built in yellow Dolphin's Barn brick, standing on the site of an older pub established in 1828. It in turn replaced an earlier inn that occupied the opposite corner. The name Yellow House does not derive from the yellow brick façades of the existing pub, but from the original building, and it is so named on John Byrne's survey map of Rathfarnham, dated 1801. Although not shown on Richard Frizell's Rathfarnham map of 1779, it was in existence by 1796,[16] on the northern boundary of a large plot of land leased by Michael Eades that stretched from where the present Catholic church stands south as far as the gateway to Glenbrook House. He also leased, with a Mrs Achmuty, the site where the present pub stands, extending from the present parish hall around the corner to the end of St Mary's Terrace. He described himself at the time as a 'Tavern keeper ... in a respectable line, and with a profitable line of business'.[17]

Many accounts of the period suggest that Eades was sympathetic with the United Irishmen, and indeed may have been a member. There is a letter, however, from Eades to the Lord Lieutenant, dated 1805,[18] in the Dublin Castle papers that seems to suggest that by that date his loyalties lay firmly with the government rather than with the rebels. In the letter Eades states that he was a Permanent Serjeant in the Rathfarnham Yeomen Cavalry since 1796 when the regiment was established, and had 'taken a very active part ...in helping to put down

---

16 N.A. OP 226/17
17 N.A. OP 226/17
18 N.A. OP 226/17

the Rebellion', and as a result incurred 'displeasure of many people, who had been formerly his friends and Customers'. Further, he had 'given his House for a Guard Room for the Yeomanry', resulting in the total loss of his business, and was unable to support himself and his wife and daughter. He asks the Lord Lieutenant to consider his case and requests a job. At the bottom of his letter is a note stating 'We know the memorialist & believe him to be a very Loyal & deserving yeoman', signed by George La Touche, commander of the Rathfarnham Yeomanry, and local landowner Robert Shaw.

It is thought that Michael Dwyer used occasionally meet Arthur Devlin, a brother of Anne Devlin, in the Yellow House when Dwyer was on the run between 1798 and 1803. The pub was also a resort for the local militia and, but for the sentiments expressed in Eades' letter, one would imagine it would have done good business during the early stages of the construction of the Military Road, during which time at least some of the two hundred Scottish Fencibles working on the road may well have spent much of their free time there.

Over the two centuries that have elapsed since the Military Road was commenced, the Yellow House has become one of the best-known landmarks in County Dublin. In 1912 it is recorded that James Joyce paused at the Yellow House with his father after a stroll in the hills. Joyce was on his second and last return visit to Ireland, and it is said that John Stanislaus Joyce, an accomplished musician, played the piano in the pub and sang a aria from *La Traviata* in which a father pleads with his son to return home. His son James, also an accomplished pianist and singer, played and sang as well, but what is not recorded.[19]

Another writer to frequent the Yellow House was Liam O'Flaherty, who was living in Wicklow in the 1930s and used to come to meet people from the city at the pub.

Opposite the Yellow House stands the Roman Catholic church designed by George C. Ashlin in what was described at the time it was dedicated in 1878 as the Early Pointed Style. The great redwoods in the grounds were planted at the same time, and now reach higher than the

---

19   See *James Joyce: The Years of Growth 1882 – 1915*, Peter Costello.

The Yellow House today

105-foot high bell tower. On the left of the entrance you will find the holy water stoup from the original Roman Catholic chapel of Rathfarnham. This was a cruciform structure with low galleries, dedicated to St Peter, which occupied a riverside site on the triangle of land between Willbrook Road and the Owendoher River, where the red brick presbyteries and the parochial hall now stand. Some traces of the old perimeter walls of the churchyard still remain between the presbytery gardens and the river, including fragments of an old wrought iron railing that may also date back to the early 1800s. In recent years a stone cross lying flat on the ground was found in the gardens of the southerly most presbytery, which is said to have marked the location of the altar of the old chapel. Local tradition has it that there was access to the chapel from a ford across the river from an old mass path that was used by the people of Templeogue. This seems very likely, because the path, looking more like a road on the 1936 OS map, sweeps in a purposeful straight line from the west, to end abruptly at the river opposite the chapel site. It is one of the few old roads in the area to have been completely wiped out, which must have happened when the Butterfield estate was being laid out in the late 1960s. The old chapel continued in use until the 1870s when the new church was erected, and after the chapel had been taken down, the parochial hall and the presbyteries were constructed. John MacDonald, whose family goes back some four hundred years in the area and who carried out building work on the two red-bricked presbyteries in the 1980s, told me that the internal back roof slope, not visible from the ground, is slated with very large, un-standard slates; one cannot help but wonder if they had been salvaged at the time of the demolition of the old chapel.

In 1781 the parish priest of Rathfarnham, Reverend Robert Bethel, was transferred to St Audoen's in the city, and a Reverend William Ledwige was appointed. He served as parish priest until his death in 1810. He lived in a house on two acres of land on the west of the Owendoher where the house called Edenbrook is shown on the recent maps, and he personally held a two-hundred-year lease at £4 yearly rent on the land on which the Roman Catholic chapel stood.[20] When he died in 1810, he bequeathed the lease to his successors, who turned out to be a wife and children, which was not entirely unusual at the time, although it did create some legal difficulties for the Archdiocese. In May 1798 Fr. Ledwige's brother was one of two rebels hanged at Rathfarnham by the militia.

A century or more later a young lad from Slane in County Meath came to work as an apprentice in Daly's Rathfarnham House in the village. Daly's was then a general grocery and hardware store, as well as a pub serving not only Rathfarnham but also the population of the

---

20 Rathfarnham Parish visitation report, July 1833.

hills to the south. The lad was desperately homesick and having endured only two days at Rathfarnham, he left abruptly and walked all the way back to his home in Slane. His name was Francis Ledwidge, and he grew up to be a significant poet before being killed in the trenches near Ypres in 1917. It is difficult not to believe that the poet was not related to the parish priest of the early 1800s.

Beyond the red brick presbyteries, the road runs parallel to the Owendoher River, only divided from it today by a curtain of shrubs and trees. Rocques map of 1760 shows that there were a number of villas on the west bank of the Owendoher River before the road from Rathfarnham to Rockbrook was built, and it is probable that new villas sprung up along it within decades. The new road, designed to carry heavy loads from the mills, would have been of a better quality than the road shown on Rocques' map running along the west bank of the river, and soon, bridges were built connecting pre-existing villas and new villas on the west bank to it. Before long the old west bank road fell into disuse, and there are no traces of it today.

One of the houses on the west bank of the river was Glenbrook, occupied at the end of the 18th century by Dr. Kirkwood, who ran the Sick Poor Dispensary. In the Rathfarnham of that time, if the poorer classes had a sympathetic employer, they could avail of a unique forerunner of private health insurance. One guinea per annum, presumably paid by an employer, entitled a worker to avail of medical care for one year in the Dispensary. The scheme not only included medical relief, but also allowed three shillings per week during a worker's illness or incapacity for work, with 'proper medicines and advice gratis'.

Glenbrook was demolished in the 1970s, but its gateway of sweeps and two piers capped in granite are still there. Today the gateway serves a pedestrian bridge which gives access to the houses that were built in the 1970s on the Glenbrook site: this bridge is built on top of the original bridge, the brick arch of which still spans the river, faced with the remains of a coat of lime plaster scored to resemble masonry.

Bloomfield was another house on the west bank and, although it is no longer there, the bridge that was built connecting it to the road is extant, but added to on the south side to provide the width to accommodate modern vehicular access. Patrick Healy writes[21] that

Glenbrook,
before demolition

Courtesy of Dublin
South Libraries

Bloomfield, an elaborate double bow-fronted, three-bay house is identified by some historians as that occupied by Thomas Addison Emmet, elder brother of Robert Emmet, during the late 18th century.

In his diaries, Wolfe Tone describes walking out to Rathfarnham with Thomas Russell to visit his friend, the elder Emmet, in April 1795:

> A short time before my departure, my friend Russell being in town, he and I walked out together, to Rathfarnham, to see Emmet, who has a charming villa there. He showed us a little study, of an elliptical form, which he was building at the bottom of the lawn, and which he said he would consecrate to our meetings, if we ever lived to see our country emancipated. I begged of him, if he intended Russell

---

21 *Rathfarnham Roads*, 2005, Patrick Healy.

The old bridge at Glenbrook

should be of the party, in addition to the books and maps it would naturally contain, to fit up a small cellaret, which should contain a few dozen of his best old claret. He showed me that he had not omitted that circumstance, which he acknowledged to be essential, and we both rallied Russell with considerable success. I mention this trifling anecdote because I love the men, and because it seems now, at least possible, that we may meet again in Emmet's study.

Patrick Healy wrote that he searched for the elliptical garden building before Bloomfield was demolished, without success.[22] Bloomfield ended its existence as Bloomfield Laundry, which closed in the 1970s, and the site was built over with houses.

22 *Archaeology, Early Christian Remains and Local Histories: Paddy Healy's Dublin*, Patrick Healy 2004.

Bloomfield as it was in the early 20th century   Courtesy of Dublin South Libraries

The stretch of road from the Yellow House to the Tuning Fork Public House was widened early in the 20th century, particularly on the east side, where housing was developed. On the west side, beyond the church hall, some stretches of the wall along the east bank of the river are original: the earliest stretches are probably those built from rounded river cobbles, sourced directly from the river below, and later stretches with the remains of a stucco render. By 1821, between Rathfarnham Road and Ballyboden, country villas such as Fairbrook, Riversdale and Edenbrook had had been built on the west side of the river, and a connection or back gate from the Ballyroan estate, originally accessed from Washington Lane, was also made.

Some 300m south of the Bloomfield bridge the Tuning Fork Public House is reached, where Whitechurch Road goes to the left and the

Military Road, called here Ballyboden Road, continues south, parallel to the Owendoher River.

Riversdale, a simple and plain house, was leased by William Butler Yeats in May 1932, and he moved in with his wife in July of that year. After the magnificence of Thoor Ballylee and his beloved Coole Park, which he frequently used as a summer retreat, it is interesting that he chose this relatively modest place to spend his last years, for it was to be his last home. It seems that the gardens there were exceptional, with a fruit garden where he went 'to share the gooseberries with the bull finches', apple and cherry trees, roses, herbaceous borders, a tennis court and a croquet lawn where he 'enjoyed playing, being good if erratic'.[23] At first he was not happy in Riversdale, which he described as a little creeper-covered farmhouse that might be in a Calvert woodcut. He missed the great trees of Coole, but once his pictures were hung on the walls of the house, he was content. Here in his study, decorated with pictures by his father and his brother Jack, illuminated by a window by Burne-Jones, he wrote many of his late poems.

In a grove of tall beech trees on the left, just before the Ballyboden Road meets the Ballyroan Road / Glendoher Road cross, there are some remains of Millbrook Mill, used in the manufacture of cloth, iron and flour at various stages during the 19th century. Close to the remains of Millbrook Mill, Seán Keating, one of Ireland's finest painters of the 20th century, built a bungalow in 1935 and called it Teach Tuadh Mumhan: he lived and worked here until his death in 1977.

On the left after the crossroads is Bolton Hall, where there was a mill operating as early as 1722, when 'the Mill and a stable joining thereto, likewise eight acres of land be ye same more or less known by name of the Seven Acres with the use and liberty of the Road leading to the said land' was rented to Caleb Smalley by William Hutchinson. A house and driveway approximately in the location of the present Bolton Hall is shown on Duncan's 1821 map, but Patrick Healy dates the present house at 1837. Some of the old mill buildings still exist on the Bolton Hall site, but are under threat from residential development.

The men who worked in the Bolton Hall mill and in the Newbrook

---

23 *W. B. Yeats*, Norman Jeffares p.310.

Riversdale in 1979

mill a little further south lived in small terraced cottages strung along the east side Ballyboden Road and at Ballyboden village, another cluster of cottages at the junction with Taylor's Lane. All of these cottages were demolished in the 1960s to make way for new council houses. Taylor's Lane is named after Alderman Thomas Taylor of Taylor's Grange, what is now Marlay, a half mile to the east. The Grange was acquired by his father, an eminent agriculturalist, at the beginning of the 18th century, and the lands passed to him after his father's death in 1727. Alderman Taylor was a prominent citizen of Dublin, and mayor at one time. Taylor's Lane is not shown on Rocques' map of 1760, but it must have been laid out very shortly after that, because the alderman died in 1763, and some time after the Grange was taken over by David La Touche. La Touche married a daughter of George Marlay, Bishop of Dromore, and renamed the estate Marlay Grange.

At the end of Taylor's Lane, in a walled demesne, is St Enda's, the house in which Padraig Pearse established his school in 1909 after moving from Cullenswood House. It was then called Hermitage, and had been built c.1780 for a distinguished Dublin dentist, Edward Hudson. Robert Emmet, through his brother who lived nearby (*see page 50*), knew the Hudsons, and he had secret trysts in the grounds of the Hermitage with Sarah Curran, who lived with her father, John Philpot Curran, in the next-door property, The Priory. The teahouse at the south-east end of the Hermitage property, where the couple used to meet, only yards from the walls of the Priory demesne, is still there today, in ruins. Edward Hudson's son, William Elliot, was born in the Hermitage in 1796 and became a successful lawyer, a member of the Repeal Association and a supporter of the Young Ireland movement. Multi-talented, he was a writer and a composer of music for patriotic songs such as 'Who Fears to Speak of Ninety-Eight', editor and financial supporter of *The Citizen*, a political and literary journal, and he subsidised the first Irish dictionary. When he died he bequeathed his library of eight hundred volumes and eighty manuscripts to the Royal Irish Academy. With these personages associated with the history of the house, the general spaciousness of the demesne and the beautiful gardens and ponds, although somewhat overgrown at the time, it is no wonder that Pearse felt the place was right for his school, which he planned to run with a high level of national and cultural idealism.

The school was a family affair, with Pearse's brother Willie teaching art, a sister, Mary, teaching music and his mother and another sister Margaret looking after matronly matters. Others who taught at the school from time to time included the poets Thomas MacDonagh and Joseph Mary Plunkett, who shared membership of the Irish Republican Brotherhood with Pearse. William Butler Yeats was a frequent visitor.

The school was in financial difficulties from the beginning, and one feels that when Padraig Pearse left St Enda's for the last time on 24 April 1916 it must have been with a certain element of relief. Local tradition has it that he cycled into town to start the rebellion, but the story that the

St Enda's School founded by Padraig Pearse

two Pearse brothers and Volunteers who had associations with St Enda's assembled at the school and marched down Whitechurch Road and along Willbrook Road to catch the tram at Rathfarnham seems the most likely. Less than two weeks later, on 3 and 4 May respectively, Padraig Pearse and Willie Pearse were found guilty of 'rebellion with the intent of assisting the enemy' and executed by firing squad. Willie had stated that he had only acted as his brother's assistant, and had not taken part in fighting, but was the only one of the sixteen who were executed who pleaded guilty to the charges.

Taylor's Lane has two other buildings of some distinction, Newbrook House, a tiny neo-gothic villa set well back from the road, and the Carnegie Library, designed by T. J. Byrne and built about 1910.

A couple of hundred metres south of the modern roundabout at Taylor's Lane the road was joined from the west by the Scholarstown Road which bridged the Owendoher River. The old bridge, originally called Boden Bridge, was replaced by the present bridge in the late 19th century, which is widely known as 'Billy's Bridge', apparently after a man named Billy Martin who lived in a hut beside it.

The Military Road from Billy's Bridge to Killakee

4

Having utilised the recently built road from Rathfarnham towards Rockbrook as the start of the Military Road, it seems that Alexander Taylor did not take the easy option at Billy's Bridge, which would have been to cross to the west side of the river and use the then existing road, now called Stocking Lane, up past Mount Venus to the Featherbeds and the open moorland. Instead, he made a decision to continue the Military Road southwards on the existing mill road east of the river as far as Rockbrook, although this meant constructing a new line of about a mile long from Rockbrook through the demesne of Killakee to reach the Featherbeds. The only readily apparent reason one can see for this is that, while the Killakee route is nearly a half kilometre longer, the longer distance reduces the grade of ascent, and the Stocking Lane/Mount Venus route has a particularly steep section as it rises past Killakee. We are so used today to effortless motorised transport that variations in road gradients are rarely noticed. Up and until horse-drawn vehicles ceased to be the common mode of transport, however, grades of climb and descent were critical. Exhausted horses, horses that died on the job and runaway carriages could make for serious complications, and there was little point in building roads that could not be used effectively. As will be discussed in more detail below, one section of the route known as the Military Road through the Killakee demesne includes an unsustainable

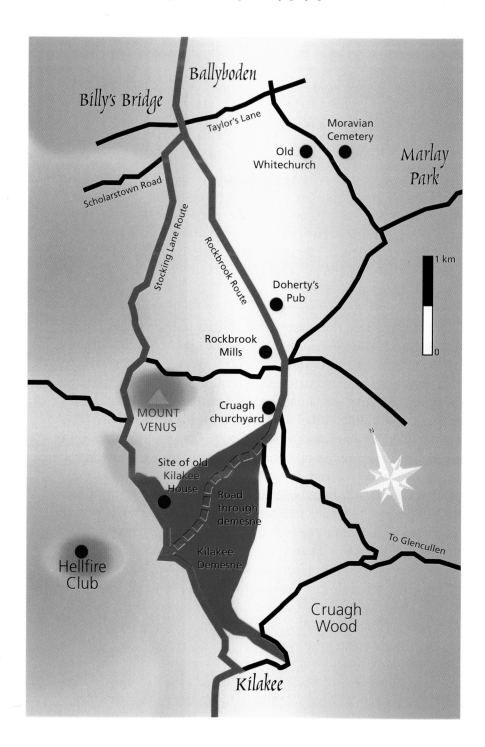

gradient of 8.85 per cent: compare this with the Mail Coach Act of 1805 which laid down a maximum of 2.85 per cent.[24] As we will see, however, the actual route on the ground through Killakee is not the line originally planned by Taylor.

It was thought for a long time that the Stocking Lane route via Mount Venus was the official Military Road. Indeed, the OS map of 1912 names the road as such, but both John Taylor's map of 1816 and William Duncan's map of 1821 clearly name the route from Billy's Bridge via Rockbrook and through the Killakee demesne towards the Featherbeds as the Military Road. On the question of which of these two routes, Mount Venus or Rockbrook, is the 'real' Military Road, I believe the evidence leans towards the Military Road being originally planned to continue up the Rockbrook road and through the Killakee demesne to reach the Featherbeds.

In February 1802, eighteen months into the construction work, Taylor reported that '6 miles of that part of the road beyond Rathfarnham which is the direct communication between Dublin and the Seven Churches in a state of nearly finished... It is now travelled upon....'[25] An examination of this statement shows it to be not strictly accurate. The actual distance from Rathfarnham to Glencree is approximately 6 Irish miles, of which almost 2 Irish miles, the distance from Rathfarnham to Rockbrook, was pre-existing. Taylor makes no mention of the fact that the section he planned through Killakee had not been completed, and according to his own c.1805 map,[26] was not even finished by that year. In fact, the actual length of road built, according to his own map, could not have been much more than 3 Irish miles. It seems clear that Taylor ran into problems with his route through the Killakee estate.

It is believed that the lands of Killakee and Montpelier Hill, which

---

24 *Alexander Taylor's Roadworks in Ireland 1780 to 1827*, Peter J O'Keefe.

25 'Report of the present state of the New Military Road now making through the mountains in the Counties of Dublin and Wicklow' 10 February 1802, NA Document Official Papers 293/1(11).

26 *A Sketch of the Environs of Dublin* by Major Alex. Taylor of His Majesty's late Royal Irish Engineers, undated but claimed by the British Library to be c.1805.

of magnitude, upon the intended Line of Road,
yet from the situation of the Ground, a great many
small Bridges, Sewers, & Water pavements, will
be required, as will appear from the Report of
that part of the Road now in progress.

I have already reported my opinion upon
the inexpediency of opening cross Roads particularly
those by Sallygap & Wicklow gap, in the letter
which I had the honour to address to you on the
22d. of August last.

It has been always in contemplation to
establish Military stations, upon the new Road
to protect the intercourse, & to command these
Mountainous communications, & I think some
are absolutely necessary.— The most proper places
in my opinion for their Sites would be the
following.   The 1st at Glencree 9 Miles from
Dublin near to the place where the Soldiers Huts
now are, & where the Roads from Sallygap &
Enniskerry meet, & go towards Dublin through
a Mile of Bog called the Featherbed, so that all communication either by Carriages or Horses, between
the Blessington, & Enniskerry, Roads, must pass
close to this post.   The situation in other respects
(is

Taylor's Report of February 1802
Courtesy of National Archives

amounted to nearly 3,000 acres, were purchased from the Conolly family of County Kildare by Luke White, a wealthy bookseller, lottery agent and financier, in 1800. White, who may have been a descendant of the Huguenot le Blanc family, invested his personal fortune in property and land, and had earlier in the same year bought Luttrell-stown Castle and demesne. Rocques map of 1760 shows a substantial settlement of buildings, possibly an extensive farm, on the west of the Killakee demesne close to the road under Montpelier or Hellfire Hill. Close to these, but a little downhill, is where Killakee House was built early in the 1800s. It is not shown on Alexander Taylor's c.1805 map, which suggests it was built later. The original line for the Military Road planned by Taylor, that shown on his 1805 map, may have been resisted by White and his son, Samuel, because it would run right in front of where they intended to build a new house. The east-facing slopes of the Killakee demesne at the time were not forested as they are now (see *Trotter below*) and there would have been an extensive panorama of Dublin and the Bay visible from the site White chose for Killakee House.

Such was White's wealth and position that he could have held up construction without being accused of obstructing the work, particularly as the Stocking Lane route was available. There are so many possibilities as to the reason why the road through the demesne was not completed as planned by 1805: Taylor was not a man to refuse financial encouragement, as problems in his later career reveal, but whatever the reason, he either exaggerated the six-mile claim in his report of 1802 or has blithely included the Stocking Lane/Mount Venus section of road in his calculations. Some suggest that the Stocking Lane name is derived from the fact that it was used by the military to supply the road project.

The impasse remained for at least five years, but subsequently Taylor probably came to an agreement with White to relocate the road through the estate on the line it takes today. It follows a low-level route

(Overleaf) An extract from Alexander Taylor's c.1805 Map showing the Killakee demesne: note that the route of the road through the demesne begins north of Rockbrook. The existing line enters Killakee south of Rockbrook.
Courtesy of the British Library

for much of the stretch, overlooked by high ground to the west, and could hardly be regarded as satisfactory from a military point of view, and has that unsustainable gradient of 8.85 per cent at the end. While this stretch may have been built by Taylor's men, and because of that was called the Military Road, I believe the Stocking Lane route was the de facto Military Road, and the stretch through Killakee, while serving as a very useful estate road, was probably never used by either the military or the public.

THE STOCKING LANE ROUTE

What is called today Stocking Lane branches off from the Scholarstown Road a few hundred metres west of the Billy's Bridge and climbs southwards into the foothills.

Some of the houses that existed on Stocking Lane and beyond in 1800, such as Hyde Park, shown on Rocques' map of 1760, have long disappeared, but between Scholarstown Road and Mount Venus Road two good houses have survived, Woodtown, which was originally called Laurel Hill, and farther on, just beyond the golf club, Woodtown Park overlooks parkland that has been little altered in nearly two hundred years: with much of its lands and gardens intact, it is a rare example of an 18th-century house complete with context to survive in County Dublin, having avoided most of the depredations of the Celtic Tiger.

This was the 'large and elegant house' with its 100-acre demesne, 'good gardens' and which he 'improved to the highest state of perfection by draining liming etc.'[27] that George Grierson moved to after 1800. He had been the King's Printer in Ireland, and had lived up until then in Rathfarnham House, near Rathfarnham Castle. He was well connected socially, and during his time there he entertained frequently. It is said that one of his house guests was Thomas Moore, who after a pleasant dinner in good company retired to the terrace, and in the balmy air of the summer twilight was inspired to write one of his most famous lyrics, 'Oft in the Stilly Night'. At the Act of Union in 1800 Grierson received compensation for the loss of his official

---

27 Statistical Survey of County Dublin, Joseph Archer 1801.

printing business (reputed to be about £100,000, a great fortune in those times), and he sold Rathfarnham House and bought Woodtown Park. He had an interest in the scientific development of agriculture, and here he began to experiment with livestock and crops. Woodtown Park did not come up to the standards of Rathfarnham House in pure architectural terms, and today it is hard to see it as 'elegant'. Much altered and added to, however, it is a good example of informal, unselfconscious organic architectural development. Grierson became well known in agricultural circles for his work, 'conducting an improvement upon the true principles of husbandry, 'folding' 200 sheep upon his farm the year through – a square yard each – shifting hurdles every night, they manure an acre every fifty days'.[28] He also pioneered the use of machinery rather than the spade for vegetable gardens, on the basis that the plough was faster and more efficient than labourers, who were likely, if unsupervised, to skip areas, throwing soil over the ground to make it seem freshly dug.

Much of the elaborate stone-built land drainage systems installed by Grierson can still be located in the lands around the house, although the designers of the nearby golf course interfered with them to their detriment. Of particular interest, though after Grierson's time, are the partially walled terraced gardens: three crescent terraces with a central path and three flights of steps lead down towards the north to a high wall which still has one glasshouse against it, a design more modest and less decorative, but very similar to that at Killakee (*see page 80*). The quality of the stonework of the steps and the piers on either side might not be as good as the remains at Killakee suggest, and unfortunately the eight great stone urns that used to adorn the piers at Woodtown Park were stolen some years ago. Inserted into the glasshouse are two exquisite fanlights from the doors of Killakee House, rescued from the ruins there by Arnold Marsh, the owner of Woodtown Park in the early 1940s.

The house was occupied from 1915 by Professor Eoin MacNeill (1867-1945) and his family, and that of his brother James. A distinguished scholar in Celtic Studies, MacNeill was co-founder with Douglas Hyde of the Gaelic League, a powerful cultural movement, in

---

28 Statistical Survey of County Dublin, Joseph Archer 1801.

1893. An article of his in *An Claidheamh Soluis* led to the Irish Volunteers being formed in 1913, and by 1916, although against the idea of political violence, he found himself Chief of Staff of that organisation. In April 1916 Irish Republican Brotherhood, under leaders such as Padraig Pearse and James Connolly, mobilised the Volunteers to bring about a countrywide rebellion without consulting MacNeill. However, he found out what was being planned and there was a frantic flurry of activity back and forth between Woodtown Park and St Enda's, Pearse's school in Rathfarnham, mentioned above, as he attempted to get Pearse and the others to call off the rising. At midnight on Easter Saturday night, convinced that the rebellion would go ahead although he had received assurances to the contrary, he placed a notice in the *Independent* newspaper for the following day cancelling all Volunteer activities. Without his order, the rebellion would have been a more widespread affair, and many who were at school in the 1940s and 1950s will remember MacNeill coming across in their history lessons as not much better than a traitor for disrupting the rebellion. Most historians, however, do not doubt that the British would have done whatever was necessary to put down the rising, and in time would have succeeded, involving the loss of very many lives. When the rebellion was over, MacNeill was arrested at Woodtown Park and taken to Arbour Hill Prison: he was sentenced to penal servitude for life for his part in it.

Further uphill past the demesne of Woodtown Park, Mount Venus Road is passed to the left. Not far past the junction, on the left, are the massive but eroded gate piers that used to serve Mount Venus House, now in ruins, some parts of which are used for farming purposes. It was built sometime in the mid-18th century, and was lived in during the 1790s by the artist James Cullen. It was another one of the properties in the area that was owned for a while by the ubiquitous George Grierson, and although much neglected, it was still habitable when the writer George Moore, in a quest for a house to rent, walked out there from Dublin on a hot July day in the early 1900s.

> ... heavy wrought-iron gates hanging between great stone pillars, the drive ascending through lonely grass-lands with no house in view, for the house lay on the farther side of the hill, a grove of beech trees

reserving it as a surprise for the visitor. A more beautiful grove I have never seen, some two hundred years old, and the house as old as it – a long house built with picturesque chimney-stacks, well placed at each end, a resolute house, emphatic as an oath, with great steps before the door, and each made out of a single stone, a house at which one knocks timidly, lest mastiffs should rush out, eager for the strangling ... wandering through a gateway, I came upon many ruins of barns and byres, and upon a heap of stones probably once used for the crushing of apples. No cow in the byre, nor pony in the stable, nor dog in the kennel, nor pig in the sty, nor gaunt Irish fowl stalking about what seemed to be the kitchen-door. An empty dovecot hung on the wall above it. Mount Venus without doves, I said. And as no answer came to my knocking I wandered back to the front of the house to enjoy the view of the sea and the line of the shore, drawn as beautifully as if Corot had drawn it. Dublin City appeared in the

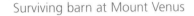

Surviving barn at Mount Venus

distance a mere murky mass, with here and there a building, faintly indicated. Nearer still the suburbs came trickling into the fields, the very fields in which I had seen herds of cattle feeding.

The great steps before the door, and the empty dovecot are no longer to be seen, and only one of the picturesque chimney stacks remains. A fragment of a curved wall, possibly a bow, faced in finely cut granite, suggests the quality of the house, while the extent of the remaining ruins, which include stone vaulted sheds, suggests the spread of the place. The only original part surviving relatively intact is a barn with a granite archway surmounted by a pediment and flanked by two tiny granite-lined Diocletian windows.

East of the ruins of Mount Venus House is Mount Venus portal dolmen, one of a number of such monuments scattered in the landscape south of Dublin, in places like Kilternan, Brennanstown, and nearby Larch Hill. The capstone at Mount Venus is said to have fallen during an earthquake in the early 18th century.

Continuing along the Stocking Lane version of the Military Road, a turn right to Tallaght is passed before the roads begins to steeply ascend the northern flanks of Montpelier Hill, probably better known today as Hellfire Hill. Look out on the left for Beehive Cottage, at the northern entrance to the Killakee estate, or what is called today Massy's Woods. The gate lodge is an exquisite little set piece, octagonal in plan, with a Tuscan column at each corner. It was in this little cottage that the impecunious last Lord Massy spent his final days. A little farther on, at the right of the road, is a long, low two-storey house, with extensive out-offices, which is called Killakee House today; much of it may have been here long before Luke White bought the land and before his Killakee House was built. This house has served in the past as a dower house and the home of the agent who managed the extensive estate of farms and lands here. The belfry you will see at the back of the house was once a common feature of large farms, and was used to call the time to the farm workers. The weather-vane on this belfry can be seen to be perforated by bullet holes: Owen Guinness of Tibradden House used it for target practice with his rifle in the early years of the 20th century. He was eventually commissioned into the Worcestershire Regiment and he lost an arm in the Battle of the Aisne in World War I. He taught at the Military Academy in Sandhurst and served again in World War II.

One of the best-preserved 18th century hunting lodges in Ireland crowns the top of 1,250-foot Montpelier Hill and has been called the Hellfire Club for many years. There is a large carpark with the sign 'Hellfire Wood' to the right of the road a couple of hundred metres past the gate lodge to Killakee House, from where it is possible to walk up to the top of the hill. The hunting lodge was built by the Right Honourable William Conolly, Speaker of the Irish House of Commons, not long before his death in 1729, in the middle of what was at the time a treeless hill in an extensive deer park. The hilltop was formerly occupied by a large cairn, probably a passage grave and Neolithic in origin, and it is said that most of the stones from this were used to construct the hunting lodge. Today, a raised part-circular earth bank with a number of kerbstones to the south of the lodge is all that remains of the cairn. When the 18th-century antiquarian Austin Cooper visited in 1779, fifty years after the hunting lodge was built, he found that the cairn still partially survived, and he describes a large stone in the centre that might have been the capstone, which suggests that the burial chamber might not, at that time, have been disturbed:

> On the top of the Hill of Montpelier stands a house built by the late Mr Conolly, it is all arched and is now out of repair. Upon the top of this hill formerly stood a cairn which was removed to make room for the house ... behind the house are still the remains of the cairn, the limits of it were composed of large stones set edgeways which made a sort of a wall or boundary about 18" high, and withinside these were the small stones heaped up. It is 34 yards diameter or 102 in circumference. In the very centre is a large stone 9' long 6' broad and about 3' thick not raised upon large stones but lying low with the stones cleared away from about it. There are several other large stones lying upon the heap. About 60 yards SW of this stands a single stone of about 5' high, but whether it is part of this Druidical Remains or only put up there for the cattle to scratch themselves I shall not positively say.

Of this last stone there is no trace today, but from Cooper's description it seems that the cairn was destroyed later in the 18th century. Before a culture of interest in antiquities began, it was common for farmers and builders to 'rob' stone from castles, cairns and other historic sites, and that probably occurred in this case. It has been suggested[29] that the larger stones were used by the military to build the Military Road bridges on the stretch of road through the Killakee estate: in at least one case, the 9-foot length of slabs used to bridge the river and the drill holes displayed on at least one of them suggest they could have originated from the single 'large stone' noted by Cooper.

It is a very exposed site and the roof was blown off during a storm not long after the lodge was built. It was replaced by a corbelled stone structure with a slated finish, a sturdy replacement that, although now without its slates, still survives, albeit damaged by a bonfire of tar barrels built upon it to celebrate the visit of Queen Victoria to Ireland in 1849.

Despite its rough appearance today, the building has signs of having been to a Palladian design and the work of an accomplished architect. Slated, rendered and with its windows and doors, it must have been an impressive sight crowning the hill. It seems likely that steps, now missing, led up to a fanlighted, main door at first floor level. The small hall inside with decorative niches on either side gave onto a staircase, probably timber, but there are no traces of it: the Office of Public Works has put in a concrete staircase in its place. The staircase led down to the kitchen and servants' quarters, and up to timber-floored sleeping accommodation over the eastern part of the building on the third floor. Off the staircase to the left and right are the reception rooms, both with large fireplaces and decorative niches and each has two great windows with views over the plain of Dublin. A return room with an arched window looks out over the destroyed cairn. On the ground floor is a kitchen with a very large fireplace, what was probably a wine cellar in the basement of the return, and a room for staff accommodation. At either end, and only accessible from the outside, are two stables; a stone-built mounting block survives at the front to assist the more corpulent guests to mount their horses. The

---

29 *Alexander Taylor's Roadworks in Ireland 1780 to 1827*, p. 67, Peter J. O'Keefe.

The Hellfire Club

building, but for its vandal-proof construction, would have been destroyed long ago, and is a mess of broken bottles and beer cans, but it is still a delight for children, and many a game of ghosts is played in its dark echoing chambers.

Although there are few descriptions of the lodge when it was being used for hunting, many stories, most of them great exaggerations, tell of the time it got the name 'Hellfire Club'. After Conolly's death, the hunting lodge was sold to Richard Parsons, the 1st Earl of Rosse, and a painter named James Worsdale. Parsons, a profligate young man who used to hold court with other young bucks such as Harry Barry, the 1st Lord Santry, and Richard 'Burnchapel' Whaley, at the Eagle Tavern on Cork Hill in Dublin, transferred some of his activities to the hunting lodge, in imitation of Sir Francis Dashwood's Hellfire Club in England.

Lurid stories of the group's excesses abounded, and one can imagine the god-fearing peasants in the vicinity locking their doors at night fearing the devil himself was abroad on the hill. These beliefs were encouraged by Parsons and his friends, who are reputed to have abducted young girls, set fire to cats, and in one case, beaten to death a dwarf whom they had lured to the place for entertainment. There is very little evidence of these activities in the press of the day, probably because of the remoteness of the place from Dublin city, and the only happening there to reach the public record is that Charles Cobbe, son of the Archbishop of Dublin, died there in July 1751. It is said that at least three deaths occurred from duelling in the vicinity. The building was damagedby fire in the late 1750s, and has not been occupied for any length of time since then.

General Holt, the insurgent leader in 1798, wrote that he spent a night in the lodge while on the run in July of that year. From his description of 'the arched room', it would appear that the timber-constructed third floor, and thus the ceiling over the eastern reception room, was still there at that date. He sent a message to his brother who lived in nearby Bohernabreena requesting some food, 'a loaf of bread, some cheese and a pint of whiskey' to help pass the time. At that time of the year it would have been a short night and, in spite of his difficulties, Holt had time to admire the beauty of the dawn he observed as the sun rose out of the Irish Sea. He wrote in his memoirs:

> I lay down in the arched room of that remarkable building. I felt confident of the protection of the Almighty that the name of enchantment and the idle stories that were told of the place had but a slight hold of my mind.
>
> I arose early the next morning, it was a splendid opening of day, I was on the very top of the hill, before me lay the country forming a regular slope to the shore with the sea in the distance, studded with

hills, Howth and Killiney, Lambay and the distant country of Fingal were just tipped by the golden rays of the rising sun with the rich and beautiful foreground full of houses and handsome residences, It was a glorious sight, and never shall I forget that sunrise.

It would be a very good thing if the landowners, Coillte, Ireland's largest commercial forestry company would consider restoring this fine historic building and turning it into a teahouse to serve the young and old of Dublin who are prepared to climb from the carpark to its wonderful viewpoint.

Below the Hellfire Club lie the extensive ruins of Montpelier House, originally called Dollymount House, a shooting lodge of Lord Ely of Rathfarnham Castle. It was built in 1763, and must have been an imposing sight with a frontage 125m long, flanked on either side by two castellated towers. In ruins today, it was last inhabited about a hundred years ago, when a poor family lived in the eastern tower. Today it is known locally as Carthy's Castle.

Back on the Military Road, there is a carpark on the left a little beyond Hellfire Wood that gives access to Massy's Woods, what remains of the Killakee demesne. About 100m farther on, at a sharp bend in the road, is the place where the Military Road exited the Killakee estate. On the right are remains of what may have been a gate lodge, behind which are the remains of the reservoir and an ice house that used to serve the great house.

THE ROCKBROOK ROUTE

From what is Billy's Bridge today, the Military Road followed the line of a pre-existing road up along the eastern bank of the Owendoher through Edmondstown towards Killakee. A surviving wheel of one of the many watermills along this stretch can be seen on the left, a couple of 100m to the south, in the midst of a modern apartment development. This wheel once served a cotton mill, which later became a laundry.

Farther on an early 20th-century factory, now disused, is soon to undergo re-development. There is a 19th-century mill behind it, and according to the 1760 map there was a substantial mill here even then. The glassless windows of the remaining buildings overlook the passing Owendoher, which, briefly tamed by massive concrete works and stone-filled steel cages, dives down deep under trees to pass by in dense shade. Beyond the factory the M50 motorway soars high across the little country road, framing the foothills ahead.

A strange-shaped house is passed on the right, called the 'Boathouse' by locals for some reason even they have forgotten. Shortly after, where the Owendoher is joined by a tributary from the east, the river and road diverge, the road continuing to ascend along a rising ridge. A drawing of the Rockbrook area as it was in 1795 by F. Jukes shows it to have been a well-organised, neat countryside at that time.

The pre-existing road here that was adopted as the Military Road served the mill at Rockbrook, the southerly-most mill on the Owendoher, the entrance to which is on the right before Mutton Lane is reached. The mill here, the extensive remains of which can be found in the grounds of Rockbrook School, was on a grand scale. From the masonry and earthworks that remain in the midst of an overgrown woodland, alive with squirrels when I passed, it is possible to interpret the ground plan of the complex, from the catchment pond, which is the area of a small lake, to the various feed channels, sluices, and return channel, a gaping hole in the ground which released the water that had done its work back to the stream, four or five metres below the works. The mill produced paper and belonged to a Mr Fry, and it was closed down at some stage before 1836, at a time when watermills were being superseded by steam mills, which did not need to be sited beside a river.

Up until recently, the 19th-century cottages of the original mill-workers' village at Rockbrook survived on the right of the road near the entrance to Rockbrook, and the early 20th-century cottages, nice little granite and yellow brick structures in which the occupants were rehoused by the local authority, are still there, a little downhill from where the original cottages stood.

Rockbrook House, at the centre of Rockbrook School, is a fine, robust two-storey, five-bay structure built about 1750 with a central

Rockbrook House

Diocletian window over the entrance door. Before it became a school, it was the home of Lord and Lady Glenavy, parents of Patrick Campbell, the broadcaster and writer.

Beyond Rockbrook the junction with Mount Venus Road is passed on the right. The house opposite used to be a police barracks, described by St John Joyce as 'a building with projecting eaves, under which the swallows have built their nests for many years past, returning year after year'.[30] Farther on, at Cruagh graveyard, the road forks, the Military Road to the right, the road to Glencullen continuing to the left. The Glencullen road probably existed as a track for centuries, following as it does the west bank of the Owendoher River up towards the gap between Cruagh Mountain and Tibradden Mountain, where it terminated at a gamekeeper's cottage high up on the side of Glendoo. The gamekeeper was employed by the Whites of

---

30 *The Neighbourhood of Dublin*, p. 150.

Cruagh Churchyard tower ⟶

Killakee, whose lands on the west bank of the Owendoher extended up into Glendoo. The track was paved and drained and extended to Glencullen between 1835 and 1840, with the assistance of a loan from the grand jury of County Dublin 'estimated at £2,100' [31] to Mr Christopher Fitzsimons, a local landowner whose seat was Glencullen House. I am sure his family connections with Daniel O'Connell may well have assisted his application for the loan. A couple of miles further on, in the heart of Glendoo, is a large boulder with an inscription commemorating one of O'Connell's 'monster meetings' that was held there.

The newer part of the Cruagh graveyard is still in use. The older section to the south is dominated by a low circular tower. Beside the tower is the ruin of the old Cruagh church, the remaining low sections of walls of which indicate that it had a nave 34 feet long. It was in use down to the religious wars of the 17th century, but it was probably a pre-Norman establishment: the antiquary George Petrie is said to have located an early Christian slab with concentric markings in the churchyard in 1816, but it has since disappeared. The tower was erected in the early 18th century to house guards to watch over new interments, at a time when cadavers fetched a good price in the medical colleges. Local historian Breda Bollard suggests that grave robbers were also after the linen shrouds or clothing of the dead, for which they would be well paid in the local papermills, which used large quantities of the material in the making of paper. Patrick Healy relates the local tradition that graveyard was the scene of skirmishes between body-snatchers and grave protectors, and that formerly the marks of bullets could be seen in the door of the tower. The earliest recorded of the ninety-odd tombstones dates from 1728, but most are well eroded and hard to read. An exception is the stone dedicated to Thomas Ambrose of the City of Dublin Brewers, which has two chubby-faced angels carved on it. There is also a stone dedicated to Mrs Mary King of New Street in the City of Dublin, who lies with ten of her children who predeceased her.

---

31 *Alexander Taylor's Roadworks in Ireland 1780 to 1827*, Peter J. O'Keefe.

Near the churchyard the entrance gates to the Killakee demesne, which St John Joyce mentions[32] as 'two massive stone pillers and a stile', stood until they were demolished in 1941 when the estate was divided.[33]

The Military Road runs along Cruagh Lane, at the end of which it enters the old Killakee demesne through a fine wrought iron gateway, passing a 19th-century gate lodge with a remarkable cantilevered roof. If you are following the route by car, this is as far as you will get, but the road can be followed today on foot through the sadly but picturesquely decayed demesne. As outlined above, the precise date of the construction of this section of Military Road as it passes through the Killakee demesne is not clear, but it must have been before 1809, when all work on the road ended.

A slight descent brings the road into the Killakee demesne on a high embankment, through which a culvert takes the Owendoher River. This embankment is clearly the work of accomplished road-builders: an old road would probably have wound down to river level and forded or bridged the river and taken a long ramp up again. The embankment ensures that little height is lost, and its construction would not have posed much difficulty to Taylor's men.

On the west side of the river the road continues uphill, the high ground to the right restrained by a well-made stone retaining wall: there are cobbles visible in the surface of the road that are no doubt original.

Luke White, who had bought the Killakee lands and the Luttrell-stown Castle estate in 1800, also bought land in County Leitrim and County Longford a few years later. His principal residence was Luttrellstown Castle and he established Lareen in County Leitrim as his country residence.[34] He was elected High Sheriff of County Leitrim in 1807 and was Member of Parliament for the county in 1818. He married twice, had ten children in all, and was well known for his charitable works. He died in London in 1824. All this activity and concentration on other properties makes it seem unlikely that it was he who built Killakee House. It was probably built by Samuel White,

---

32 *The Neighbourhood of Dublin*, p. 150.
33 *Rathfarnham Roads*, Patrick Healy, p. 74.
34 *If Those Trees Could Speak*, Frank Tracy, p. 29.

Killakee House c.1890
Courtesy of the Architectural Archive

his second son and the inheritor of the Killakee estate, who, although he took over from his father as High Sheriff of County Leitrim in 1809, was apparently living at Killakee from early in the 1800s, most probably in the old Killakee House.

The house that White built was a two-storey, five-bay structure with a Tuscan-columned entry porch on the east, and large three-windowed bows on the back and sides. It was sited on an eminence overlooking a series of garden terraces, with a fine view of Dublin Bay.

The site is so heavily treed today it is difficult to imagine clear views of the Bay, but a description of the house and gardens in 1864 by the garden designer William Robinson[35] makes it clear that the views to be had at the time were considerable:

---

35 *Gardeners Chronicle*, 1864, p.117.

> The house is built near the top of the hill ... and literally looks down on Dublin and its environs for miles around ...to the north could be seen the mountains of Mourne ... to the east, between the Park and the sea, lay the fair city of Dublin itself ... were charming views of the hills of Killiney and Dalkey, with as good a bird's eye view of the Kingstown Harbour as of Dublin.

It is likely that it was Samuel White who began to develop the gardens of Killakee, planting flowering rhododendrons and exotic trees when the new house was completed, and eventually commissioning the designer Sir Ninian Niven to carry out considerable improvements some time after 1838. Niven was born in Scotland in 1799 and came to Ireland around 1825 as the gardener to the Chief Secretary for Ireland, Lord Glenelg, in the Phoenix Park in Dublin. In 1834 he was appointed Director of the Botanic Gardens at Glasnevin, but a few years later he resigned to set up as a landscape designer and gardener, styling himself 'Professor of Landscape Gardening'.[36]

Niven, who also designed the gardens of Santry Court and Templeogue House in Dublin, Kilkenny Castle and Baronscourt, County Tyrone, laid out on this County Dublin hillside two formal Victorian gardens of gravel walks, terraces, solemn rows of Irish yews and Chilean Arucaria or monkey puzzles, and statuary. The house overlooked a terraced garden, down which a six-metre wide flight of twenty-four steps led to a rose garden. The main feature of the rose garden was a granite-edged fountain with at its centre a rustic plinth, topped by a bronze statue of Neptune in a chariot of shells drawn by sea horses.

Down in the valley, ten minutes' walk from the house, another garden was laid out, a vast walled enclosure sited alongside the river that flows through the glen. The walled garden was arranged on three terraced lawns. The topmost lawn had figures of Venus and Diana surrounded by tightly clipped Portugal laurels. The second terrace had figures of Sappho and Flora, while on the third stood a range of domed and vaulted glasshouses by Richard Turner, in front of which stood a

---

36 *A History of Gardening in Ireland*, Lamb and Bowe.

Lower garden and glasshouses at Killakee
Courtesy of the National Library of Ireland

pair of carved granite fountains. At the northern side of the great wall against which the Turner glasshouses were built, a large fernery was constructed.

Many of the exotic trees planted in Killakee's halcyon days so long ago survive and have been labelled by Coillte, which now owns the demesne. Niven was fond of redwoods and you will find examples of the Californian Coast redwood, one of the world's most famous and impressive trees, and also the tallest. Its normal home is a narrow strip of Pacific coast from the Canadian border to southern California, and while the tallest recorded tree tops out at 110m (367 feet), it is not unusual for them to reach 80m. Redwoods like these can live to a great age; in California many of the older trees are four hundred to eight hundred years old, and there are veterans of over two thousand years old. The Bhutan cypress is normally found in the eastern Himalayas

Killakee gardens today

and southern China, where it grows at elevations of 1,500 to 2,700m and often reaches 30m in height. Another Himalayan species you will find in Killakee is the Deodar Cedar, which is normally found in the western end of the range and in Afghanistan, where it reaches heights of 55m at altitudes of up to 3,000m, more than three times higher than Ireland's highest mountain.

The White estates passed into the ownership of nineteen-year-old John Thomas Massy of County Limerick in 1853, although Killakee remained registered to Samuel White's widow, Ann White for her lifetime. After his brother's death in 1874 Massy became the 6th Baron Massy, and in 1880, when Anne White died, he inherited Killakee House and 3,422 acres to add to the estates he already had, including 8,568 acres in County Limerick, 24,751 acres in County Leitrim and 1,120 acres in County Tipperary. In 1881 the rents from his lands netted Baron Massy about £12,000, which in today's money would amount to something over one million euro.[37] Although he spent most of his time at his residence in Castleconnell, County Limerick, he used Killakee for shooting parties. Large numbers of guests, together with their servants, were accommodated and wined and dined for days on end, shooting grouse, woodcock and snipe on Cruagh and Glendoo mountains. Massy also held house parties during the Dublin Horse Show, the Punchestown Races and the 'Season' festivities in Dublin Castle.

Rental income from land began a severe economic decline in the 1880s, and much of the Massy lands were sold. Poor investment of the monies received cut the Massy income further, at a time when the maintenance and running costs of his properties in Limerick, Leitrim and at Killakee, along with the cost of the extravagant lifestyle being carried on, were soaring. By the time of John Thomas Massy's death in 1915, he was hopelessly in debt. His grandson Hamon Massy moved into Killakee House in 1919, but as the affairs of the Massy family went from bad to worse in the early 1920s, he was evicted by the bank, and although he succeeded to the peerage in 1926 on the death of his father, Hamon Massy was reduced to living in the tiny gate lodge of Killakee House, called Beehive Cottage, supported by his wife who had a job in the Irish Sweepstakes.

The bank eventually put a caretaker into Killakee House and sought to sell the house and lands. By 1941, no purchaser having been found, the house was sold to a builder, who removed the slates, roof and floor timbers and anything else that could be recycled, and demolished the rest. The gardens and the demesne in general fell into dereliction.

While some of the big trees have survived, nature has taken over everywhere else, reclaiming the territory wrested from it by Samuel

---

37 *If Those Trees Could Speak*, Frank Tracy, p. 46.

Beehive Cottage

White nearly two centuries ago. What survived destruction by man in the demolition of buildings and removal of stone has been taken over slowly, powerfully and inexorably by nature in the sixty years since. Rank grass and scrub has grown over the paths and lawns, and sprouting trees have colonised the walls, upending formal granite steps and toppling piers. In the midst of it all, only a palimpsest of the gardens survives, the most significant being the brickwork 'back-end' of the conservatories, where what is left of the system of irrigation canals and ponds for the fruit trees and exotic shrubs can still be made out against a great retaining wall perforated with gothic openings. In the foreground, the scant remains of the curved base of Turners great conservatory can be found. The decaying brick walls of these gardens, destabilised in places by laurels and sycamores, are the most substantial evidence of the glory that once was Killakee. The place is darkened by the many trees there today, even in winter, but you must remember that when Niven's garden was at its best only a limited number of carefully placed, selected redwoods, cypresses and monkey puzzle trees broke the sky, allowing the sun to flood the valley.

The stump of the wonderful Neptune fountain and the curved granite surround can still be seen, together with one of the two great monkey puzzle trees described by William Robinson back in 1864, in the garden of a house built in the last few decades on the site of the great mansion. There are also vestiges of the balustrades, terraces and retaining walls. Scattered about in the undergrowth along the old driveway are pieces of the old wall, and fragments of limestone columns and plinths.

Killakee was eventually taken over by the Forestry Department, and the demesne is today open to the public, but apart from a considerable amount of new planting, nothing has been done to preserve sparse remains of the grandeur that was.

At the southern end of the demesne, the track through the lands that was once Taylor's aspirational Military Road reaches the boundary at the Killakee end of the Stocking Lane road, and here the two routes that have been named the Military Road join again.

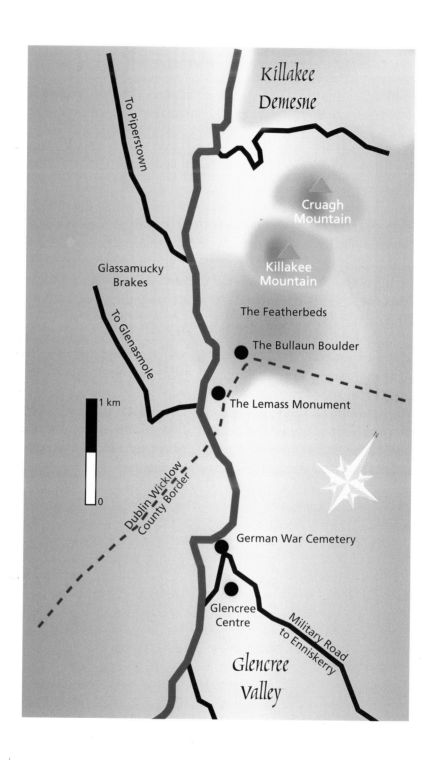

Killakee
Demesne

To Piperstown

Cruagh
Mountain

Glassamucky
Brakes

Killakee
Mountain

To Glenasmole

The Featherbeds

1 km

The Bullaun Boulder

The Lemass Monument

0

Dublin Wicklow
County Border

N

German War Cemetery

Glencree
Centre

Military Road
to Enniskerry

Glencree
Valley

From Killakee to Glencree

5

From the southern end of the Killakee demesne, what was not more than a bog road used by shepherds and peat cutters in 1800 wound up the last hundred metres onto the northern Hanks of Killakee Mountain, or White Sands Mountain as it was then called, and eventually petered out. This bog road would have needed considerable upgrading to bring it up to the standard of a military road, and between where it ended and Glencree a completely new road was required. Where the road comes out of the trees there is a viewing place that overlooks Dublin Bay. In clear weather the coastline can be seen extending northwards to the Mourne mountains, 70 miles away, and the whole of Dublin City and its suburbs and great bay are laid out below. In really good conditions, the summit of South Barrule on the Isle of Man peeks its head above the horizon to the north-east. While on a walking tour through Wicklow in 1814, John Trotter described the view from here as it was then, much the same as seen by Taylor's soldiers when they brought their roadworks to this point:

> From hence we beheld a beautiful and extended plain at our feet studded with villas, noble mansions and cottages. Here and there a river winded to the sea. Woods were interspersed, and fertile fields of grain. The delightful Dublin Bay, covered with many white sails of vessels, going and returning, terminated by the picturesque small mountain of Howth, – the peninsula, and thickly inhabited coast, near Dublin, – charmed the eye. Its blue and glossy surface seemed that of a lovely lake! The pigeon-house and lighthouse stretched far into it, and the animated appearance of commerce enlivened it in every part. The Black Rock, Dunleary, and Dalhey,[38] with its

---

38 Dalkey, which cannot actually be seen from the point he mentions.

venerable island, bounded it on the right. At its extremity stood the city of Dublin, sending forth the smoke of early lighted fires, and having all the appearance of a great and wealthy emporium.

From the viewing point at Killakee, the Military Road winds on uphill, climbing more gently now through modern forestry, and comes out of the trees to reach the high moorland called the Featherbeds and one of the finest views in the Dublin Hills opens up to the right and ahead. The long, deep valley of Glenasmole, the Glen of the Thrushes, with the two reservoir lakes glinting at its heart, nestles below: on the far side of the valley rounded mountains step up gently southwards towards the highest summit in the Dublin range, Kippure, topped by a tall television mast.

The moorland called the Featherbeds is an area of blanket bog that stretches 4km southwards to the valley of Glencree. It is bordered on the east by Killakee Mountain, named Whitesands Mountain on the early maps, and the valley of Glenasmole on the west. To connect Glencree to the top of the bog road at the end of Stocking Lane, Taylor had to build the road across the 4km of peat. The moorland here has been covered in peat for thousands of years, and we can assume, from the existence of bog roads on Rocques' 1760 map, that the peat around the fringes had been well harvested for fuel, down to the boulder clay that lies below it. The rights to the peat belonged to the landowners, but it is certain that the peasants would have taken what they could, when they could: every winter there was a severe shortage of fuel among the poor cottagers. 'The fuel of the lower class', Archer wrote in his *Statistical Survey of County Dublin* 1801, 'is a scarce article in this county; some turf is to be had in different parts of the range of mountains from the Scalp to Tallaght, and a small portion to the north; in other parts, the hedges are demolished without mercy, and, in many places, they gather the dung about the fields and even burn straw.'

Where peat-cutting had not yet intruded into the Featherbeds, Taylor had to deal with depths of one to two metres of peat in constructing his road, getting his first taste of the high moorland landscape that was to dominate much of the rest of the Military Road

Glenasmole from the Featherbeds

route ahead. His experience in the Highlands of Scotland must have now come in useful, and although he was not an engineer, he showed considerable engineering skill in the various specifications he used for the peat land sections of road.

There is no contemporary written specification for the construction of the Military Road over peat land. It is thought by some that a 'corduroy' method was employed, that is, excavation followed by the laying down of a bed of timber logs, on top of which layers of stones were compacted, and the surface finished in gravel. A local sheep farmer told me that he saw the road opened up some years ago in an area of bog, in places as deep as 4m, and that the base of the road was filled with tightly packed bundles of rushes. Whether trees or rushes, it is clear that in the peat bog environment without oxygen, organic matter will not rot and, if well compacted, should be sustainable. From the longevity of most parts of the road, it seems that Taylor was imaginative and resourceful and used a range of specifications, utilising readily available materials to suit particular conditions. Stone from granite outcrops was plentiful under the peat for the whole length of the road, and broken up sufficiently and compacted well, it would have been ideal for a road base. Taylor does not seem to have been put off by the depth of peat: if he had been, he would not have adopted the plan of rigorously following the contours as he did, rather than be biased by the depth of peat in particular areas, which could have been measured by rods. The alternative of cutting through hillocks and building causeways across valleys may well have been considerably more time-consuming. His rigorous adherence to contours can be seen everywhere along the moorland sections, particularly south of the Sally Gap and on the descent towards Glenmacnass waterfall.

A critical aspect of Taylor's road construction method across peat land was the drainage system he adopted. Good drainage was fundamental to keeping the base courses stable and to prevent them from being washed out, so in places he would have laid a wide network of drains, some up to 30m wide, along the road route to serve his 4m-wide road, and where a stream was encountered, he had robust culverts and bridges constructed, most of which are still serving today.[39]

Robert Fraser reported in his *Statistical Survey of Wicklow* in 1801, referring to the road, 'By the scientific ability with which it is conducted, it is likely to be a very durable improvement, as well as a most useful road ...' and that the drainage system used by Taylor was already providing inspiration for the value of draining bogs 'rendering them consistent, and capable of bearing people on their surface in those places where before they were impassable'. The northern part of the road was in place for more than a dozen years when Richard Griffiths, in his report accompanying his Map of Wicklow for the Bogs Commissioners, mentions that 'the admirable manner in which it [the road] is executed may serve as a model for all mountain roads'.

Although there have been a few cases of subsidence over the last two hundred years, most of the road has remained intact, and the

---

39 *Alexander Taylor's Roadworks in Ireland 1780 to 1827*, Peter J. O'Keefe.

proof of the success of Taylor's design can be seen in the usage the road gets today, taking traffic of a volume and weight far beyond anything that could have been conceived of in 1800.

Commencing work in August 1800 when the peat bogs would be at their driest, Taylor's men would have had about two to three months of suitable weather before winter slowed up the work, and it can be assumed that good progress was made on the Featherbeds section of the road. When the weather became inhospitable on the high moorlands, it is possible that Taylor sent his men down to the more sheltered sections to continue work, and in this way some of the Fencibles may have been billeted out in Ballyboden, carrying out upgrading on the existing road. Similarly, the Sally Gap group could have been sent down into Glencree to assist the group working on the Enniskerry spur. From the documentation available, it would seem that the Featherbeds section between Killakee and Glencree was completed in the summer of 1801.

Early in 1801 Prime Minister William Pitt resigned his position over the king's refusal to support his proposals for Catholic Emancipation in Ireland. Charles Cornwallis, champion of the Military Road, resigned in sympathy, because he believed that the pacification of Ireland depended on two main factors, namely the abolition of the Irish parliament and Catholic emancipation. His work in Ireland had been difficult, and it must have been with some relief that he sailed back to England, although he felt, after all his efforts, that Ireland remained in an unstable condition. In April 1801 the Royal Corps of Engineers of Ireland was disbanded, but Alexander Taylor retired from the army as Major Taylor, having been promoted from Captain before the end of the same month, no doubt with the departing Lord Lieutenant's assistance.

The name Featherbeds comes from the dramatic display of bog cotton (Eriophoretum) that used to characterise the place before extensive turf-cutting began in the 18th century, and as this activity has almost entirely ceased, the plant is slowly coming back into its own.

(Overleaf) The Featherbeds

On the tops of almost all the mountains you can see from the Featherbeds are prehistoric cairns of the Neolithic period, and on Seahan itself, the highest summit on the far side of the valley, the Neolithic cairn is surrounded by a series of Bronze Age cist graves. On nearby Seefin the stone lintelled entrance to a passage is exposed, and one can squeeze through to reach the chamber, open to the sky since it is said to have collapsed in the same earthquake which brought down the Mount Venus dolmen (*see page 68*). It is probable that communities of Neolithic people lived on these mountaintops, their dwellings gathered around their burial monuments like a village around a church. More recent examples of this form are common throughout hilly areas all over southern Europe, where climatic conditions are probably similar to what prevailed in Ireland nearly five millennia ago.

The landscape of the Featherbeds and the surrounding mountains have such a look of permanence that one has to remind oneself that the bogs were not always here. Up until three or four millennia ago the surroundings would have been mainly mountain woodland, the evidence of which, in the form of roots and trunks of ancient trees, can be seen in places at the base of the peat. Some 1.5km to the north-west of the Featherbeds, overlooking Glenasmole, is a low eminence called Piperstown Hill, on the southern slopes of which no less than fifteen prehistoric sites were exposed some years ago when a severe heather fire stripped all herbage off the hill. Eight of the sites proved to be burial cairns; the remaining seven were habitation sites, the majority of which dated from the Neolithic or about five thousand years ago. Most of the remains of timber found on the sites were oak, a species which mixed with pine and birch would have filled the valleys in this area at that time. On the mineral soils of higher ground, up to 460m under Kippure, stumps of pine trees have been found under cutaway bog that date back at least 4,200 years, and pollen studies suggest that birch was also present at these high altitudes.

In front of me as I write there is a pyramidic piece of oak which I cut from a large tree base at the bottom of the peat near Lough Bray. The outside, exposed surfaces are black-streaked silver-grey, but the new cuts are golden brown in colour, and the growth-rings are prominent. The extent of the remaining tree base, no more than a metre across, suggests that it did not survive to grow to full size, but was subsumed and preserved by the peat before it could do so. When I look at this piece, I not only imagine how the mountains looked at the time that it grew. The tree rings of the fragment of wood record eight years of the tree's life, during which it stood under a sun that also warmed Phoenicians as they traded throughout the Mediterranean, Assyrians and Babylonians as they fought in the time of the biblical conqueror Nebuchadnezzar, and Rameses II as he watched the erection of the Great Temple of Abu Simbel.

In this area of Wicklow the peat cover began to develop about three to four millennia ago and the stone cairns on the summits of Seefin and Seefingan can clearly be seen to have been built before this, on the original ground level at the base of the peat cover. On the saddle between nearby Seefin and Seefingan, pollen extracted from cores of the soil at the base of the peat some years ago indicated that a decline in elms and pines was followed by the appearance of plantain, evidence that indicates tree clearance was followed by farming on this high land in Neolithic times before the bog began to develop. The climate then was milder, and the thin soil of the mountains would have encouraged only sparse forest, so the trees would have been easier to clear to create pastures, compared to the lowlands, which would have been covered with a thick, impenetrable, malarial swamp and wildwood. Only a reliable supply of water would have been needed to make settlements possible on these summits. There is a spring just below the summit of Seahan,[40] and with the help of a friend who is a douser or water diviner, I have ascertained that there is also a water source under the peat near the cairn on Seefin.

Evidence of a non-physical kind that the area has been inhabited for many millennia can be found in the ancient sagas and legends of Ireland. The sheltered valley of Glenasmole, overlooked by these mountains, features prominently in the epic tales of Finn MacCumhaill and the Fianna, which are so outlandish that one feels they must be based on a series of real happenings, however unrelated the happening might be.

---

40 *The Neighbourhood of Dublin*, St John Joyce, p. 146.

Passage Tomb on Seefin

One story tells of Finn, his companions and his two famous hounds, Bran and Sgeolan, hunting a piebald doe for an entire day without being able to catch her, until, as darkness fell, they found themselves lost among the hills that surround the valley. As they rested, a beautiful woman appeared and invited them all to a feast, which of course, tired and hungry as they were, they were delighted to accept. After the feast they were resting when a hideous Grecian witch appeared on the scene and, admiring the physique of Finn, asked him to be her husband. Finn, however, refused and the witch was so enraged that she promised to invade Ireland and kill them all. While Finn and the Fianna, Ireland's standing army, were kept in the hills above Glenasmole in a spell and in the thrall of fifty amazons, she gathered her fleet and invaded Ireland. Just as she was about to defeat

96

Lemass monument

the Irish King at Howth, the Fianna broke the spell and launched themselves on the invaders, killing them all, including the witch and the amazons. One truly wonders from what occurrences and over what time span this tale was concocted. In another story Finn battles with and kills the Arrach or Dragon of Glenasmole.

The two reservoirs in Glenasmole were constructed in the 1880s, Victorian engineering ingenuity ensuring that the upper one would supply sufficient drinking water to the township of Rathmines, while the lower would ensure that the mills along the course of the River Dodder had a guaranteed supply of water. In the mid-1840s the Dodder supplied two distilleries and twenty-seven mills, including flourmills, woollen mills and paper mills, one of which, the Jefferson Smurfit plant at Clonskeagh, is still in place. Along the course of the river also, and using the valuable water in turn, were five iron foundries, a sawmill, a calico printing works, a cotton-spinning factory and a cutlery mill.

At the southern end of Glenasmole the little hamlet of Glassamucky, 'the Green of the Pigs', surrounded by hills tinted in heather-purple and bracken-brown, has hardly changed in a century. Nearby, embowered in rhododendrons and mountain ash at the head of the glen, is Glenasmole Lodge, built originally as a hunting lodge by George Grierson.

Just beyond the forestry above Killakee a road to the right is passed which leads down to Piperstown; it existed as a bridle track at the time of the Rocques' map in 1760. The Military Road climbs gently onto the broad heather-covered moorland that slopes down westwards from the insignificant summits of Killakee Mountain and Glendoo Mountain, 539m and 582m respectively. Today the well-surfaced road brings frequent traffic, but not too many years ago very few vehicles and even less pedestrians ventured beyond Killakee. The walker J.B. Malone wrote of his first foray into the Featherbeds in August 1933, as follows:

> There are at least three routes to Glendalough, but for walking, the Military Road is the best. It is the shortest (25 miles approx), it runs roughly due south, and since it is the highest road in Wicklow, it provides the nearest approach to 'ridge walking' that a road can give. By the Military Road there are only five horizons between Dublin and Glendalough. My first horizon that day was bounded by the Dublin Mountains, constantly looming larger as I went forward, till at last, having past the woods at Killakee, I came to the beginning of the Featherbed, where desolation abruptly begins. Before me lay the Six Mountains, clear against the cloudless sky, and bounding the second horizon. After eating a little, and looking back over the city and the Bay, again I went forward.

Turf cutting on the Featherbeds began in earnest in the 18th century, and a great increase in harvesting took place in the Featherbeds and Sallygap area during World War II, when thousands of city dwellers,[41]

---

41 *The Bogs of Ireland* Feehan & O'Donovan 1996.

starved of coal imports, took to the hills to cut their own fuel. Many of them were exiles from parts of Ireland where turf-cutting was a common everyday affair, and for many it was the beginning of a family tradition that survived for thirty or forty years.

> How beautiful the bog, said Camier.
> Most beautiful, said Mercier.
> Will you look at that heather, said Camier.
> Mercier looked with ostentation at the heather and whistled incredulously.
> Underneath there is turf, said Camier.
> One would never think so, said Mercier.
>
> SAMUEL BECKETT, *Mercier and Camier*

During the Emergency, turf-cutters found many artefacts in or under the bogs in the area, which indicates that people there were at least passing by here in former centuries. They included a 250mm-long bronze dagger, a pre-Christian wooden vessel and a weaver's comb made of horn that dated to the Iron Age.

When John Wood, an English walker, passed this way in 1947 he remarked:

> No house was in sight, but people were numerous, for besides roadmenders there were many busy diggers of turf, and nearly everyone I passed greeted me with a request for the time. It was not much after three o'clock when I was first hailed with 'Good evening' and startled I looked at my watch, but in the next week or two I found that evening is any time after three in the afternoon and occasionally even earlier. The salutation 'Good afternoon' I never heard at all, and 'Good day' seemed to be the usage between noon and three.

As recently as the 1970s, as many as 500 people from the city had leases for turf-cutting on the Featherbeds. Interest in this time-consuming and energetic method of providing domestic fuel waned, however, as Ireland gained in prosperity and younger members of families, a very necessary part of the labour force, became less inclined to spend their leisure time on the bogs. One old peat-cutter I spoke to blamed the drop-off on natural gas, which came onstream in the late 1970s as an economical fuel for central heating. Since that time the Wicklow National Park has taken over these lands, originally part of the Powerscourt estate, and as leases expired they were not renewed. As the Featherbeds return to a natural moorland state, the bog-cotton which gives them their name is beginning to spread again.

No evidence has been found to show that this high plateau was inhabited at any stage in the past, but while the surrounding moorland looks relatively featureless, careful observation will reveal a number of interesting features. In places below the road you will find circular patches of vegetation of a different colour to that around. These are the remains of ice-pits, relics of the pre-refrigerator age. In the 19th century the big houses and the hotels of the city of Dublin had a need for ice in summertime for the preparation of desserts and drinks. They obtained it from a number of small contractors in the Dublin foothills, who built stone-lined pits into which they packed snow in the winter-time, which, protected by a straw thatch which insulated the pit and kept the rain out, preserved the resulting ice well into the following summer, when it was cut into blocks and transported down into town. The circular patches you see are some of the more basic types of these 'icehouses'. Remains of the more elaborate stone-lined icehouses can be found beside the road down to Piperstown.

The highest point of this part of the Military Road (480m) is reached a kilometre after emerging from the forest. To the left, 50m in from the road, is a monument marking the spot where the body of Noel Lemass, a Republican unofficially executed by the Free State Government forces, was found in 1923, after the Civil War had officially ended. He had been arrested in the street in Dublin in June of that year and it was not until October that someone with sympathy for the family quietly gave the location of the body to his mother at their shop in Capel Street. In 1927 a passing Londoner, Gladys Hynes, wrote the following spontaneous poem about the grave in the visitors' book of McGuirk's Teahouse, 3km farther along the road.

Lemass'es Cross [sic]

By the lonely mountain road stands a cross of stone
It marks where a bullet-pierced body lay, unknown,
While day followed night and night followed day,
And the quiet mountain folk passed by on their way,
And were long to learn
What horror lay hidden there under the fern,

But surely the Earth of Ireland was wiser and knew,
And bade the heather and fern bow down as they grew,
And hushed him in stillness there to peaceful rest,
While like a child he lay close to her breast.

To this, a later note was added on the same page of the visitors' book, 'They that live by the sword, die by the sword', alluding to the rumour of the time that, although his mother maintained he had no part in military activities during the Civil War, Lemass was the unofficial executioner of the Republican forces. His younger brother, Seán, was to become Taoiseach from 1959 to 1966, when he was a pivotal figure in ushering the country into the modern age.

The Lemass monument cuts into a low mearing bank that can be discerned crossing left and right of it. Built during the 18th century in stone and now covered with mountain herbage (it is marked as 'New Mearing Drain' on Rocques' map of 1760), it marks the boundary between the counties of Dublin and Wicklow. If you follow the bank from the Lemass monument through the rough heather to the left or north, it will take you to a change in direction in the boundary, where the bank makes a sharp ninety-degree turn towards the north-west. Marking the corner is a great, flat-topped granite boulder with three shallow basins in its top. It looks as if it has lain here since the beginning of time. It is not possible to say for sure whether the basins are a natural phenomenon or if they were bored into the boulder by man. I would guess, however, in an open location like this where they could not have been formed by flowing water, it is likely that they are man-made, but for what purpose we may never know. One way or the other, this rock must have had some considerable significance in prehistoric times, when any unusual rock would have received particular attention, and certainly a well-known landmark for centuries, marking as it does this corner in the Dublin-Wicklow boundary.

Well in from the road to the east and south of the county boundary, there is a grassy oasis, about an acre in extent, in the middle of the peat bog. Some remains of earth and stone banks border it and within it there is a raised level platform with traces of stone walls. This is what remains of an old hunting lodge of the La Touche family of Marlay.[42] Careful study of the surrounds will show what seems to be an earth and stone bank walled 'avenue' leading southwards. To the east is a place called Garryduff, which means black garden, indicating that the place may have been inhabited at some stage. It is intriguing to imagine that the name might go back to the time before the bog, and has something to do with the bullaun boulder mentioned above.

After the Lemass monument there is another turn off to the right leading down to Glassamucky. A little further on, a long straight gravel bog road leads off into the moorland to the left. The junction here was the location of much of the 1952 movie *The Gentle Gunman*, starring Dirk Bogarde and John Mills, and with Barbara Mullen, Eddie Byrne and Jack McGowran also taking part. For the movie, a two-storey cottage and a garage with a petrol pump were built on the side of the road opposite the long bog road, roughly where the barrier is today. The story told of dark intrigues in the IRA during World War II, with stiff upper Irish lips, love triangles and betrayals. The movie ends with a four-car chase up the bog road, dust flying and guns blazing. The buildings were removed after the filming, but I am told that an old bus that also appeared in the film remained here on the side of the road for a few years after, serving tea to the large turf-cutting community that spent many hours on the bogs from spring to autumn.

The bog road was built in 1940 along the county boundary, on the Dublin side according to the OS map, to access peat bogs under Kippure. It runs for 1.5km to reach the Mareen Brook, after which the old mearing bank continues almost all the way to the top of Kippure, making it an easy way to navigate to the summit of the mountain. At the end of the bog road a moated site was recorded by the early

The Bullaun Boulder

Ordnance Surveyors, which it has been suggested was[43] the location of the legendary hostel Da Deargas. The hostel was said to be on the ancient road down through Wicklow, the Slighe Cualann and the

---

43   Article by Henry Morris in *Journal of the Royal Society of the Antiquaries of Ireland*, 1937, p. 313

legend tells of King Conaire Mor, King of Ireland, staying there overnight while on a trip south. The lights of the hostel were spotted by pirates sailing past along the Wicklow coast, and they came ashore and made their way across country to attack it. The king and his entourage put up a good defence, but the pirates won the fight and the king was killed. Whether or not the moated construction found under Kippure was the site of the Da Deargas hostel was a matter of much discussion and argument by Celtic scholars for many years in the early 20th century. Although at 460m it is quite high above sea level, it is 15km from the coast, and there would have been, at best, only a tiny sliver of visibility from the sea between the high ground of Knockree and Prince William's Seat, so it seems unlikely to me. At the bog road, the Military Road crosses from County Dublin into County Wicklow.

Above Glencree, on the western flanks of the hill called Knocknagun, is a rock called Castle Toole in the 1830s by Eugene O'Curry of the Ordnance Survey, that has an IHS motif carved on it. There is no local tradition, however, that this was used as a mass rock, and it is possible that this carving, along with a number of others that can be found on the rocks of the stream that flows into the valley here, were made by one of the brothers from St Kevin's Reformatory. Above it on the summit is another substantial tor, as big as a house, un-named, except it just might be the 'great rock Karaght Lobayne' mentioned in a record of 1592.[44]

The Military Road has been descending again since it passed the Lemass memorial, and at the southern edge of the Featherbeds, it reaches the valley of Glencree.

---

44 Calendar of Archbishop Alen's register *c.*1172-1534: prepared and edited from the original in the united dioceses of Dublin and Glendalough and Kildare, C. MacNeill (ed.), (Dublin 1950) – all quoted in *Dublin City and County – From Prehistory to Present*, p.185.

G lencree is a five-kilometre-long valley extending out of the
mountains eastwards to the lowlands of the coast, where a
last remnant of the woods that covered much of the Wicklow
mountains survived up until medieval times: the local place name
Lackandarragh[45] means 'the Slope of the Oaks', suggesting that oak
trees were the dominant species here. By the time of Henry II,
woodlands all over England were coveted as hunting grounds by
royalty, and not long after the Normans gained a foothold in Ireland,
the oak wood at Glencree, because of its proximity to Dublin by way of
the coast, was set apart as a Royal Deer Park. In 1244 eighty deer were
sent from the Royal Forest at Chester to stock the King's Park at
Glencree, and it is possible that some form of ditch and bank was
constructed as a park boundary, because the term 'park' usually
suggests an enclosure. It may be that the low, eroded bank that today
forms part of the border between counties Dublin and Wicklow and
which runs along the ridge of Knocknagun and Prince William's Seat[46]
to the north of the valley is older than presently thought, and was once
part of this boundary enclosure.

The historian T. P. LeFanu described Glencree as follows:

> ...and indeed it must have formed a beautiful park when clothed in
> dense wood stretching along by Ballyross and the steep hillsides of
> Crone, away up to the bald crest of Maulin, and the black, peaty
> moorland of Tonduff; diversified by the lighter green of the birches

---

45 *The Placenames of County Wicklow V*, Liam Price.
46 Named for Prince William, son of George IV, who accompanied his father on
his visit to these parts in 1821 and is said to have climbed to this viewpoint.

of Bananagh and the hazels of Ballicoyle, and broken here and there by the grey rocks of Ballyreach, the green glade of Cloon, the foaming torrent of Aska Bawn, flashing down to the river forks of Ballylerane, or the white head of Knockbawn rising above the oaks of Lackandarragh.[47]

The next valley to the north, Glencullen, belonged to St Mary's Abbey in Dublin, and it seems that the abbot and monks were known to stray across into Glencree: records show that in 1291 the abbot was accused of hunting in the Royal Forest 'with nets and other engines, and with greyhounds, and of taking wild beasts and working his will with them, to the great injury of our lord the King'.[48]

Up until the early Norman period the oaks of Glencree forest would have been a relatively untouched remnant of post glacial wildwood, made up of trees, which, owing to their great age, would have been of huge size compared to modern trees. Irish oak was generally known for its durability and superiority over English oak and as early as the 11th century, even before the Norman invasion, it was specified by William Rufus, son of William the Conqueror, for the roof of Westminster Hall in London. As royal hunting waned towards the end of the 13th century, interest in the use of forests like Glencree for the supply of oak for construction purposes increased. Records show that in 1285 the Dominican Friars of Dublin were granted fifteen oaks from Glencree for the building of a church, and a few years after St Thomas's in Dublin was granted twenty, and William Burnell, constable of Dublin Castle, was granted twelve oaks to build his house. In 1290 Eleanor, the wife of Edward I, established a large sawmill at Glencree to supply the timber to build her castle in Haverford in south Wales. It is likely, at the time, that the required timbers were sized and cut on site rather than attempt to export entire trees, which logistically would have been impossible. By the time the Wicklow clans advanced north and Glencree became a disputed territory once more, it seems that most of the original forest of great trees had disappeared.

---

47 RSAI jn Ser 5 Vol. III 268-80 1893.
48 RSAI jn Ser 5 Vol. III 268-80 1893.

By the early 17th century Glencree was in the hands of Sir Richard Wingfield, who became Viscount Powerscourt in 1618, and it remained in Powerscourt ownership until the late 20th century.

When the Military Road was being planned, it was decided that blockhouses or barracks would be located along it at regular intervals to fortify it. The architect for the barracks was a Mr John Gibson, and although I was not able to track down the actual plans, if such still do exist, we know that he produced two alternative designs and the Lord Lieutenant chose 'Plan No. 1' as being the most appropriate.[49] The land on which the barracks were built was leased from the local landowners.

There were originally four barracks along the road, at Glencree, Laragh, Drumgoff and Aghavannagh, and a fifth in the Glen of Imaal at a place called Leitrim. It is said that consideration was given to a sixth where the Military Road crosses the Liffey under Kippure, but I have found no documentary evidence for this, although one at the Sally Gap is mentioned in the earliest documentary reference I could find to the barracks, recommendations by Alexander Taylor in a letter attached to his report dated 10 February 1802 on the progress of the Military Road.

'It has always been in contemplation to establish Military Stations, upon the new road to protect the intercourse, to command these mountainous communications, and I think some are absolutely necessary. The most proper places in my opinion for their sites would be the following. The 1st at Glencree 9 miles from Dublin near the place where the soldiers Hutts now are, and where the Roads from Sallygap and Enniskerry meet and go towards Dublin through a Mile of Bog called the Featherbeds, so that all communication either by carriage or Horses, between Blessington & Enniskerry Roads must pass close to this point. The situation in other respects is favourable, being sheltered from the north and west winds by a ridge of high ground. The second place most proper to command the communications, would be the Sallygap, where the new road crosses the one from Blessington to Roundwood, but this

---

49 Kilmainham Papers, Vol. 17. Letter, Beckwith to Wickham, 3 January 1803.

situation is high and much exposed to the North and West, and rather too near the first station, being only 5 miles distant.

He suggested a third barracks at Laragh near Glendalough, 10 miles from the Sally Gap, the fourth at Glenmalure, 5 miles from Glendalough, and the fifth at Aghavannagh, 4 miles from Glenmalure. He says that although these positions are closer than would be usually necessary, in this 'most disaffected part of the country' the suggested proximity was necessary. In the end, the barracks at Sally Gap was not built, but his advice on the other locations was taken up, and early in 1803 sites were acquired along the route of the Military Road at Glencree, Laragh, Drumgoff and Aghavannagh, and construction started later in that year. It seems that Taylor had little more to do with the barracks after preparing his recommendations, other than the construction of access roads from the Military Road, and the work of building the barracks was carried out by civilian contractors. As mentioned, another barracks was built at Leitrim in the Glen of Imaal, some miles west of the Military Road, to allow a permanent army presence in that disaffected area.

The barracks at Glencree, built on land leased from Lord Powerscourt, was completed by 1806, when in July Lord Wellesley, the future Duke of Wellington, had breakfast there with the Barrack Master, Captain Barry, and Major Taylor. It was initially garrisoned by a troop of seventy-five soldiers. At the end of the Napoleonic Wars, garrisons were reduced to a sergeant and a few men, who acted more as caretakers than as a garrison, and by the 1820s the army had left Glencree. The Wicklow Constabulary occupied the place until 1834, after which it was only intermittently occupied for a variety of uses, including for a period a base for the surveyors of the Ordnance Survey.

The view of Glencree Barracks by the geologist artist George Victor Du Noyer shown overleaf is as it was in the 1840s. It depicts the place as it was without trees and shows the dramatic drop away into the Glencree River. Much of the fortified perimeter wall is shown, but it was almost completely removed during later construction work in the second half of the 19th century. From the drawing it is clear that the eastern perimeter wall of the barracks ran close to the eastern façade

Glencree Barracks c.1840
Courtesy of Royal Society of the Antiquaries of Ireland

of the building, probably along the high point of the terrace that exists there today. The entrance gate and access road are shown in the location they remain today. In spite of the promontory site dominating the ground to the east, north and south, the barracks was clearly overlooked by the high ground to the west.

What is clear about this view is the absence of the Captain's House, as it is called locally, just across the road from the barracks. Much about the house suggests it is early 19th century, and tradition has it that it was Captain Taylor's house, built at the time of the erection of the Fencibles' small town of huts. Du Noyer was a very accurate observer and draughtsman, however, and the absence of the house in his drawing suggests that it must have been built later, and therefore could not have been Captain Taylor's house.

The fact that the barracks, although in dilapidated condition, was still barely habitable in the 1850s was instrumental in bringing about a transformation of the western end of the valley, which up until then had consisted of mainly very poor land and 'rocky heathy pastures'.

In the wake of the Great Famine, poverty and deprivation were widespread in Ireland, and inevitably for many of the poor, survival involved petty crime. There was a great increase in juvenile larceny of money, clothes and food, and it was normal for apprehended juvenile

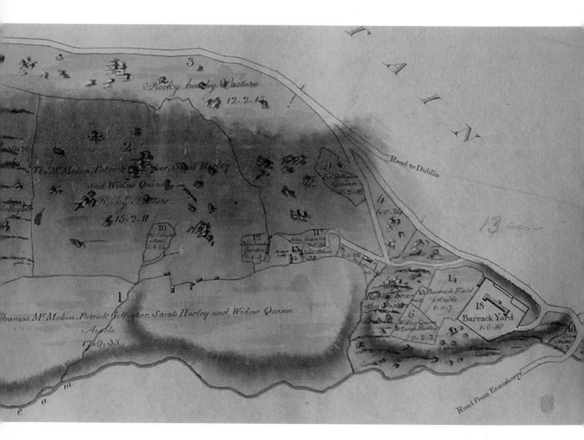

The head of Glencree valley in 1816: much of the landscape can be seen to be 'rocky heathy pasture'.

'criminals' to be sent to prison. There, apart from the obvious dangers, they came under the influence of hardened adult criminals, and most were doomed to continue a life of crime after release. In 1853 there were 12,000 children under the age of sixteen years sent to prison by the courts in Ireland, and of those about 2,000 were under the age of ten years.

To address this problem, the Irish Reformatory Schools Act was enacted in 1858, and the Oblates of Mary Immaculate, a Roman Catholic order of priests and lay brothers, were asked to set up a Reform School to cater solely for juvenile offenders. The old barracks at Glencree was the chosen location for the establishment: it was in very poor condition, but the brothers spent the summer and winter of 1858 carrying out the enormous task of making the place habitable. St Kevin's Reformatory was opened in April 1859, and the first child was admitted the following month. By the end of the year there were ninety-four boys enrolled, and within a few years there were three hundred. Over the next twenty years the Oblates, assisted now by an army of youngsters, transformed the barracks and the landscape of the head of the valley. Prodigious work was carried out clearing, reclaiming and cultivating 100 acres of poor land, using the boulders from the clearance to build substantial boundary and field walls. These walls can be still seen today, and one wonders not only at the engineering skill involved, but the sheer brute strength required to erect them. A reservoir was constructed to supply the domestic and industrial needs of the establishment, and additional dormitories, a refectory, workshops and eventually a chapel were built, most of the labour, including the fitting out of the buildings, being provided by the boys.

The task that the Oblates set themselves was to train the boys in their care in a variety of trades and occupations, so that when they were released, they would have the possibility of making a decent living, rather than returning to crime. Industrial teachers were employed to teach the boys trades such as cabinet-making, shoemaking, upholstery, stone-cutting, plumbing, baking and even knitting. After a few years the shoes and clothing of the boys and the staff were made entirely by the inmates, and they were almost self-sufficient in food, growing their own vegetables and providing their own beef and mutton from the herd of cattle and over two hundred sheep they kept on the mountain.

It must have been a hard life for the boys: coming as they did from either the slums of the cities or the miserable bothans of rural Ireland, most of them were probably undernourished and in chronic bad health. The new regime of fresh air, regular meals of simple but good food, and constant exercise must have, for most of them, ensured a steady improvement in their physical and mental condition. With regard to their treatment, Fr. Fox, the manager in 1866, wrote in the annual report for St Kevin's the manner in which the boys were dealt with:

Firmness tempered by kindness, good wholesome food, limited only in quality, warm clothing though it be poor is essential. The gentle nursing if they are sick, fatherly reproof when it is deserved, the word rather than the blow, the smile oftener than the frown: these are qualities that will gradually bring even the most hardened criminal to understand that the institution is not a place of punishment but a refuge and a home.

They were hard times, however. In the winter of 1870 a Dublin lad called Bernard Young, sentenced to Glencree for larceny, barefoot and in rags, died from exposure in the back of a prison van while being brought to Glencree. What did not emerge at the time, but was passed down by the people of Glencree, was that the two Dublin Metropolitan policemen who had brought the boy from the city had stopped at a sheebeen just above Glencree, and it was while they were inside warming themselves that the boy died in the van.

The Irish alpinist John Healy, walking the mountains as a young man, described passing along the Featherbed section of the Military Road in January 1916 as follows:

> It was close under the trees but when we emerged on to the Featherbed it became cool. The upper part of Seechon was covered with mist and when we saw the whole Kippure chain in the throes of black clouds, we began to suspect that Kippure would slip out of our reach again. A very definite line demarcated the region of the mist from the valley below. The latter looked very clear and sharp in details. The Military road was in very bad condition. When approaching the top of the pass we were surprised to hear the sound of a brass band. Soon we came in sight of it on a bend of the road beyond and below us, and it was accompanied by a long line of dark figures behind. Such an appearance in the mountain solitudes, together with the unearthly sounds of the band that were interrupted and modified by the gust of wind, might well have been regarded as a supernatural visitation. It was like a bit of one of Poe's tales (a Tale of the Rugged Mountain?).
>
> On passing this awe-inspiring battalion we found that it consisted of the young criminals of Glencree Reformatory.[50]

---

50 John Healy's diaries.

Glencree Reformatory c.1900
Courtesy of the National Library of Ireland

Claude Wall was shown around the reformatory in 1924 by one of the brothers who had 'a considerable amount of his dinner adhering to his face and waistcoat'.[51]

St Kevin's Reformatory was closed in 1940, when the staff and boys moved to the less climatically challenged location of St Conleth's Reformatory School in Daingean, County Offaly, which had been in operation since 1870.

Glencree remained in Oblate hands for a few years afterwards and for a while in 1943 was used as a Novitiate, before the buildings came into the ownership of the wartime Ministry for Supply.

The buildings were unoccupied until the end of World War II,

---

51 NL Acc. 5150, Claude Wall's diaries.

when, under the auspices of the Irish Red Cross, they were opened up again for the reception of young refugees from Poland and Germany, en route to the Irish homes that were to foster them. What was called Operation Shamrock, run mainly by the Red Cross, began in 1946 when the Department of External Affairs agreed to accept five hundred German children for fostering in Ireland. In July of that year the first children, eighty-eight in number, arrived; by October, one hundred and ninety children had come, of whom one hundred and thirty-four had already been placed in foster homes.[52] The majority of the children, aged between three and fifteen, were from the mainly Catholic Ruhr area. Some were orphans, but many had parents who, in the aftermath of the war, were simply unable to look after them.

The children to be fostered were taken first to Glencree, and it must have been tough there that year, as it was a harsh winter. In Glencree they were kept under medical observation and built up with a nourishing diet – in some parts of Germany there were still severe food shortages. When they were strong and healthy, they were fostered by Irish families from all over the country. Although all the foster homes were inspected before the children were fostered, little was done to ensure that recipient families were suitable for the children they took, and distribution was a little haphazard, with the children being simply lined up for selection. A former foster child, Ursula Weber, recalled:

> As twins, we were determined not to be separated. I saw a kind-looking woman and pulled her sleeve. She immediately said she would take me. I pulled my sister towards me. The woman looked at us and nodded.[53]

French Sisters of Charity ran the centre for the Red Cross and also brought over young French children for respite holidays in summer-time. John Wood, walking from Dublin to Glendalough in 1948, gives the following description of reaching Glencree:

---

52 *Germany and Ireland 1945-1955* – Cathy Molohan, Irish Academic Press, 1999.
53 *Germany and Ireland 1945-1955* – Cathy Molohan, Irish Academic Press, 1999.

Glencree Barracks today

Beyond the watershed the pleasant Glencree opened up to South-eastward, and near the road junction an old man held me in conversation, which soon became a complaint against the reception locally of French and Polish children for recuperation after their wartime privations whilst some foods were still rationed in Ireland. He thought the sugar ration of 12oz. weekly was just about enough for one day, but I told him it was half as much again as we got in Britain, and asked if it were not in accordance with his religion to feed these lambs. I gathered from his rambling rejoinder that Christian teaching was all very well so long as it was kept in the chapel – an attitude that has its supporters in Britain, too. A little later I saw a large party of boys and girls, evidently both French and Poles, ambling along behind a nun, and even had a brief conversation in my halting French with a lad from Paris. Among these mountains a few weeks later a French aircraft crashed in dense mist, and about twenty young girls who were coming to Ireland on holiday suffered severely (as did the crew) shock, exposure and in some cases injuries. What is surprising is that such wild country should be less than an hour's motor ride from a capital city. In the Balkans you would accept that sort of thing, but it is unexpected in western Europe.

When John Huston filmed parts of the movie *Sinful Davy* in Wicklow in 1967, he skilfully transformed the old reformatory into the period Scottish town of Stirling. He laid down a concrete road along which a stagecoach was to be driven at speed, but not satisfied with the sound of the horses' hooves, he borrowed almost an acre of cobblestones from the Dublin Corporation store and laid them on the concrete to get the correct sound. The cobbles were never returned: most of them were removed during later drainage works, but the concrete road and some of the cobbles can still be discerned.

After the 1940s the buildings at Glencree were silent again for many years, until in September 1972 the Office of Public Works offered the place to an organisation called Working For Peace. They wanted to set up a reconciliation centre to deal with the conflict in Northern Ireland and provide refuge for people caught up in the violence. Again, gargantuan works were carried out to resurrect the buildings, and the Glencree Centre for Reconciliation was born. Over the next twenty years the centre ran work camps, North-South exchange holidays, holidays for refugee families and residential courses in conflict resolution, peace and non-violence. The contribution that the centre made to the peace process in Northern Ireland has been widely acknowledged, and funds were made available to enable the centre to be expanded in 1998. It became a flagship of co-operation between the British and Irish governments, and both countries committed funds to the ongoing work of the centre. So, after nearly two centuries, a building built by the British for war-like purposes has been rebuilt by the British and Irish and dedicated to peace. There is an exhibition centre, coffee bar and plenty of parking in the Centre and the public are welcomed.

Just north of the Glencree Centre is the German Military Cemetery, a sensitively landscaped garden of remembrance for one hundred and thirty-four Germans who either died in Ireland during the two world wars, or whose remains were washed up on our shores.

Those buried in the cemetery are mainly Luftwaffe aircrew who died when their damaged aircraft crashed in Ireland, and Kriegsmarine personnel who died at sea and whose bodies were washed ashore. There are also the graves of forty-six unfortunate German civilians who had been detained in Britain at the start of the war and were being transported to Canada when their ship was sunk by a U-boat off Tory Island in July 1940. Six of the graves are of soldiers who died in captivity in a British prisoner-of-war camp in Ireland during World War I. At the back of the graveyard is a monument depicting a carved sword wrapped in barbed wire, commemorating the German spy Dr Hermann Goertz. From early in the war ,Goertz, who had already spent some time spying in England, trained to parachute into Ireland to make contact with the IRA and to obtain their assistance in the invasion of Britain. At a party in Berlin in early 1940 Goertz met Francis Stuart, the writer, who was lecturing in university there. When Goertz alluded to the fact that he would be 'visiting' Ireland, Stuart told him that if he had any problems, he could call into Laragh Castle in County Wicklow, where his wife, Iseult, lived.

The saga unfolded from there on as a comedy of errors. Goertz parachuted at night into County Meath in May 1940, coming down near Ballivor, seventy miles away from where he intended to land. A second parachute with his radio, a shovel and other bits and pieces went astray, and Goertz was unable to locate them in the dark. Thus, immediately in trouble, he decided to head south for Laragh, nearly 70 miles away. He swam the river Boyne at night on the way, during which operation he lost more of his spy kit, including his invisible ink pad. He still had some British currency, which he did not realise was acceptable in Ireland, a map, a plan for bringing arms to Ireland by submarine, a list of possible anti-de Valera contacts, and, for sentimental reasons, his medals from World War I were sewn inside his coat.

He must have been a hardy man for a fifty-year-old, because he covered the distance to Laragh in four days. Iseult immediately took him in, fed him and sent him to bed. While he slept, she took the bus to Dublin, where she bought him a few suits of clothes in Switzers. Thus readied for his spying mission, with the help of Jim O'Donovan,

German War Cemetery

an IRA activist, he was launched into Emergency Ireland.[54]

For eighteen months he eluded escape. He was by far the most successful German agent: most of the other nine who landed in Ireland were captured within weeks and sometimes days. Goertz was finally captured in December 1941 and interned for the duration of the

---

54 *The Shamrock and the Swastika* Carolle J, Carter, Pacific, 1979

war. After the war Goertz wanted to remain in Ireland and was offered asylum here in September 1946. He went to work as Secretary of the Save the German Children Fund, an Irish relief organisation for German refugee children, but his freedom was short-lived. In April 1947 he and the other internee spies who had settled in Ireland were arrested, and sent to Mountjoy Jail. The British government had decided that former agents should be deported back to Germany where they could be thoroughly interrogated, and for some reason, de Valera acquiesced. Goertz claimed that he would be imprisoned in Germany and, since he was then fifty-six, would probably spend the rest of his life in jail. He pleaded for asylum. His pleas were ignored, but before the authorities could deport him, he committed suicide.

The German cemetery at Glencree was dedicated in 1961 and the bodies, which had lain in fifteen different counties until then, were brought together and re-interred there.

The old quarry in which the graveyard is located was probably opened originally for stone for the Military Road in 1800 and for the construction of the Barracks in 1803. More stone was removed in the mid-19th century by the Oblate brothers for the additional buildings needed by the Reformatory, and for the steps and terraces of the gardens at Powerscourt House.

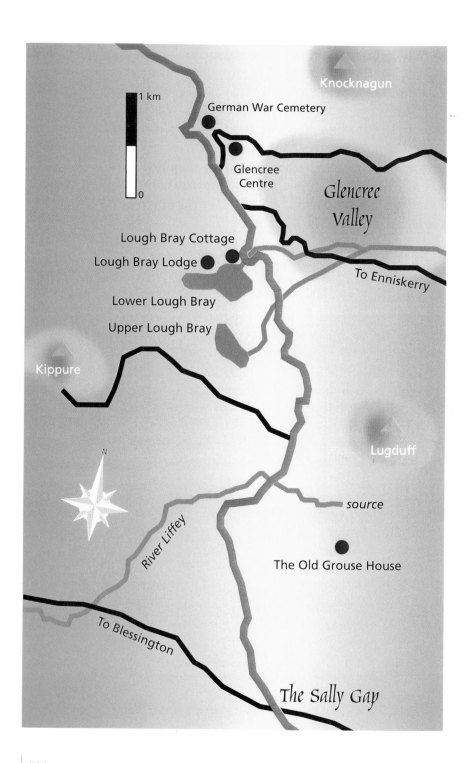

Knocknagun

1 km

German War Cemetery

0

Glencree
Centre

Glencree
Valley

Lough Bray Cottage
Lough Bray Lodge

To Enniskerry

Lower Lough Bray

Upper Lough Bray

Kippure

N

Lugduff

source

River Liffey

The Old Grouse House

To Blessington

The Sally Gap

Glencree to the Sally Gap   7

A s mentioned previously, Alexander Taylor was not an engineer by training. He had trained, or served his time, as a surveyor, and was employed in his first job as such in Scotland in 1768 at the age of twenty-four. Two years later he was carrying out land surveys for the Duke of Gordon, using a theodolite, an instrument that, although under development since the early 18th century, was still an advanced piece of technology.[55] From then until 1800 Taylor seems to have worked busily as a surveyor and mapmaker. Nowhere, however, have I been able to find any reference to Taylor studying or serving his time at civil engineering, and there is no question but competence in that profession was essential to the success of the planning and construction of the Military Road. I have come to the conclusion that the thirty years accumulated experience in surveying that Taylor had at the time of the building of the Military Road gave him the wisdom to seek out and rely upon expertise that he did not possess. Although we know little about the three subalterns assigned to him and the experienced masons provided by the Duke of York's Fencibles from Banffshire and the North Cork Militia at the start of the project, we have to assume that the technical success of the road is due to a combination of Taylor's experience and leadership and their expertise.

The route of the Military Road south out of Glencree was such that this engineering expertise was required in three locations over the first mile. Two bridges were required to take the road across mountain streams that could have had significant flows in wintertime, and a large retaining wall was required to take the road up and past a rocky

---

55 *George Taylor, a Surveyor o' Pairts*, Imago Mundi No. 10 1975, Dr. I. H. Adams.

Bridge draining Upper Lough Bray

promontory at the north-west side of Powerscourt Mountain, east of Upper Lough Bray. These three examples of Military Road engineering are extant, and can be admired today. The first bridge, over the stream issuing from Lower Lough Bray, is a simple enough affair, but the second one, built to direct the waters of a larger stream issuing from Upper Lough safely under the road, is a complex, skewed affair. The stone for the retaining wall and the large volume of fill required for the road came from a large quarry opened on the spot, one of the biggest of the many roadside quarries used in the construction of the road. The quarry today fulfils a contemporary need by providing a carpark for hill walkers and those visiting the lake below.

Before the road begins to climb south out of Glencree, a gateway is

Lower Lough Bray and Lough Bray Lodge

passed on the right. It leads to Lough Bray Lodge, a summer villa that was originally built by a Dr Philip Crampton[56] in 1826, evidence of how pacified Wicklow had become in the preceding twenty years. It was accidentally burned down a short time later. A replacement was

56 Sir Philip Crampton (1777-1858) was surgeon general to military forces in Ireland and at one time a physician to Queen Victoria. He was one of the founder members of the Royal Zoological Society of Ireland and was instrumental in having the site for Dublin Zoo granted.

erected in about 1830 to the designs of William Morrison, who had three years earlier carried out alterations to St Valery near Bray, for Crampton's brother. The new cottage combined, in Morrison's words, 'the Swiss cottage style ... with the old English cottage'. He exhibited a model of the cottage at the Royal Hibernian Academy in 1832. The design has strong similarities with the alterations designed for a house called Carpenham, built by Morrison in Rostrevor, County Down for a Mr Hamilton, brother-in-law to the Duke of Wellington, around the same time; the architect was known to use very similar designs, as if attempting to perfect an idea.[57] The cottage has been considerably added to and the original intricate and decorative half-timber walls were unfortunately plastered over late in the 20th century.

The rebuilt cottage was a gift to Crampton from the Duke of Northumberland, who had acted as ambassador-extraordinary at the coronation of Charles X, and was Lord Lieutenant of Ireland for a year. The Halls recount[58] that the Duke 'spent some happy days with Sir Philip in this romantic spot' and, it is said, was in occupation of the cottage when the destructive fire occurred. Another reason offered for the generosity of the gift is that Crampton had cured the Duke of a 'skin complaint'. The tranquillity of Glencree has made it a resort of writers for many years, and in the 1960s writers Frederick Forsyth and Lee Dunne spent sojourns at Lough Bray Cottage.

A little beyond the gateway to Lough Bray Lodge is a small cottage, the last habitation on the Military Road before the valley of Glenmacnass. For about a century and a half it and an earlier cottage on the same site was the home of the McGuirk family, who were Powerscourt tenant farmers in Glencree at least as early as 1816. Some time in the late 19th century the wife of one of the McGuirks began to augment the family income by running a teahouse in their tiny thatched home, which became known as Lough Bray Cottage, and at 1,200 feet, was the highest

---

57 Dr McParland writes: 'Once decided on a formula, Morrison tended to stick to it, even at the risk of being dangerously repetitive; having devised an original and satisfactory villa plan, he was prepared to use it and elaborate it frequently.'

58 *Hall's Ireland*, Mr & Mrs S. C. Hall.

teahouse in Ireland. It was certainly a significant landmark when long-distance walker H. C. Hart passed on one of his marathons in December 1884, even if he was not prepared to waste time by stopping to take refreshments. His note describing his trek says:

> Sunday Dec. 7 1884. Left Terenure at quarter past eleven; fort at Ballinascorney gap at half twelve; Signpost at Coronation Plantation at two thirty – Sallygap where roads meet three thirty – Lough Bray Cottage four forty. Terenure a quarter to seven. No stop. From half twelve to half six it blew a gale and rained in torrents. Time seven and a half hours, 34 miles.

The teahouse soon became a popular halting point for the occupants of coaches, charabancs and early touring cars, as well as for pedestrians and cyclists. Remarkably, two further generations of daughters-in-law of the original Mrs McGuirk continued the business into the second half of the 20th century. It became a tradition to keep a visitors' book in which customers were invited to sign their names and write comments on the fare they had enjoyed, and this tradition was still being carried

McGuirk's cottage today

on when the teahouse finally closed in 1996. Seven volumes of these remarkable books have survived, and through the signatures, comments and drawings they contain, they provide an unique insight into the evolution of the social history of Ireland over the period and include the names of many who were involved in the political and cultural development of the new Irish State. In the early days it is clear that 'touring' was a pastime of the well-off who had names such as W. W. Carruthers or Mr Seagrave McCormick, and visitors often could not resist giving one's 'position' as well as one's name, as in 'N.C. Geoghegan, Attorney Gen. Dublin' who visited in August 1898, or 'C.J. McCarthy PRIA City Architect', who had tea in July 1902.

Many well-known names appear during the first half of the 20th century, including art collector Sir Hugh Lane, surgeon and writer Oliver St John Gogarty, poet Austin Clarke, botanist Robert Lloyd Praeger and novelist L.A.G. Strong, while poet Denis Devlin contributed verses and Harry Kernoff and Seán O'Sullivan are among those who left exquisite pencil sketches. William Beckett, father of the writer and playwright Samuel Beckett, is also there: he brought his son many times into the mountains and frequent references to the surrounding landscape appear in the playwright's work.

After the original Mrs McGuirk's son, Tom, married, her daughter-in-law assisted her in the teahouse, and she eventually took over, providing, according to the visitors' comments, good fresh produce and excellent tea that was very much up to her mother-in-law's standards, in spite of the lack of space in the two-room cottage.

Glencree was a favourite place for the writer John Millington Synge. His friend Frank Fay, the actor and critic, had a house down in the valley and they frequently took walks and pony-trap rides up to McGuirk's teahouse. He wrote in *In Wicklow and West Kerry*, published in 1921:

> This morning the air is clear, and there is a trace of summer again. I am sitting in a nook beside the stream from the Upper Lake, close down among the heather and bracken and rushes. I have seen the people going up to Mass in the Reformatory and the valley seems empty of life.

Sketch of Harry Kernoff by Seán O'Sullivan in McGuirk's Visitors' Books in 1928

Sketch of Seán O'Sullivan by Harry Kernoff in McGuirk's Visitors' Books in 1928

Both courtesy of Tom McGuirk

I have gone on, mile after mile, of the road to Sally Gap, between brown dikes and chasms in the turf, with broken footbridges across them, or between sheets of sickly moss and bog-cotton that is unable to thrive. The road is caked with moss that breaks like pie-crust under my feet, and in corners where there is shelter there are sheep loitering, or a few straggling grouse ....The fog has come down in places; I am meeting multitudes of hares that run round me at a little distance – looking enormous in the mists – or sit up on their ends against the sky line to watch me going by. When I sit down for a moment the sense of loneliness has no equal. I can hear nothing but the slow running of water and the grouse crowing and chuckling underneath the band of cloud.

When his future wife, Molly Allgood, rented Lough Bray lodge in the summer of 1907 Synge boarded with the McGuirks to be near her. His poem 'To The Oaks Of Glencree' starts like a love poem and, like much of his writings about the Wicklow Mountains, soon develops a more sombre tone:

> My arms are round you, and I lean
> Against you, while the lark
> Sings over us, and golden lights, and green
> Shadows are on your bark.
>
> There'll come a season when you'll stretch
> Black boards to cover me:
> Then in Mount Jerome I will lie, poor wretch,
> With worms eternally.

The cottage the McGuirks lived in at the time of Synge's visit was a tiny, two-roomed thatched place, and one wonders at how little space there must have been when Synge was there. He slept on a 'press bed', a rudimentary bed stored in a kind of wardrobe kept in an alcove beside the fireplace. Tom McGuirk, the last member of the family, now residing in Canada, told me that he remembers it as being just a sheet of canvas stretched over a wooden frame, with crosspieces about every foot and no mattress, so it must have been very uncomfortable. Toiletry arrangements consisted of a bucket. He said the bed was thrown out about 1957 when they gave up keeping overnight guests.

Synge wrote the following description of an evening at McGuirk's in *In Wicklow and West Kerry*:

> There is a dense white fog around the cottage, and we seem to be shut away from any habitation. All round behind the hills there is a moan and rumble of thunder coming nearer, at times with a fierce and sudden crash. The bracken has a nearly painful green in the strangeness of the light. Enormous sheep are passing in and out of the skyline.
>
> There is a strange depression about the cottage tonight. The woman of the house is taken ill and has got into bed beside her

mother-in-law, who is over ninety and is wandering in her mind. The man of the house has gone away ten miles for medicine, and I am left with the two children, who are playing silently about the door.

The larches in the haggard are dripping heavily with damp, and the hens and geese, bewildered with the noise and gloom, are cackling with uneasy dread. All one's senses are disturbed. As I walk backwards and forwards, a few yards above and below the door, the little stream I do not see seems to roar out of the cloud.

Every leaf and twig is heavy with drops, and a dog that has passed with a sad-eyed herd looked wet and draggled and afraid.

Tom McGuirk told me that his father, Arthur, who was about nine years old at the time, was one of the two McGuirk children playing silently about the door, and remembered the particular evening. With reference to Synge's lines, he told Tom that his mother wasn't sick at all, but climbed into bed because she was mortally afraid of thunder and lighting, and his father remembered Synge leaning out the open window to watch the storm and his mother being terrified the 'gintleman would be struck dead'. Tom said his father was also afraid of thunder and lightning, and at the slightest hint of a storm, he would be off to his bed. The larches mentioned were cut down in the 1950s. When Arthur married, his wife Mona, Tom's mother, in turn moved in to help with the teahouse. It cannot have been easy for her—her mother-in-law is said to have been a formidable woman—but in fact people in the valley still talk about Mona's bread, so she obviously carried on the tradition very well, taking over after the second Mrs McGuirk died in 1942.

They must have been handsome women, all three of them, as is evidenced by the frequent comments in the visitors' books which drew attention to more than the quality of the food.

James Woods, having walked from Rathmines on Stephen's Day 1899 wrote 'Enjoyed our lunch here and glad to see our friend Mrs McGuirk so blooming.' In April 1902 Rev. C. Shanks of Bray wrote 'Mrs McGuirk looking A1 as ever and reminding one as ever of old times, while as for her daughter-in-law, least said, or rather written, the better, as we hear "Tom" keeps a gun handy and *can* shoot, even

St John Gogarty's natural table with its flat top! ———▶

around corners.' R.J. Fallon of 16 Altona Terrace, North Circular Road, Dublin wrote in October 1906: 'Came to see Mrs McGuirk and partake of a cup of tea which was as beautiful and refreshing as the fair lady who dispensed it.' By 1940 visitors were still full of praise: in March of that year Tom Adamson 'had a lovely egg and met a sweet lady' and Louis and Mollie O'Reilly 'enjoyed a delicious tea and a long chat with our loved old friend'. A few days later, Mr and Mrs James Halpin wrote 'If Hitler comes, let's hope he samples Mrs McGuirk's tea, home-made and fresh egg as we did, to our complete satisfaction.' It is also clear from the visitors' books that rationing did not reach into the Wicklow Mountains: in March 1941 Joe Groome from Bray ate '3 eggs, 6 rashers and drank 8 cups of tea!'

The physician Bethal Solomon was a regular visitor and when Mona was pregnant with Tom, Dr Solomon asked her to come into the Rotunda for the birth, which she did. Mona died about 1962.

Touring Ireland on foot in 1947 John Wood stopped at the cottage for tea on his way to Glendalough and described the place:

> The mass of Kippure terminates suddenly in a granite cliff, under which the lower Lough Bray lies hidden from the nearby road. An adjacent cottage was the one I had been seeking, for I was told in Dublin that it was the only tea-place I should pass, and I was more than ready for a meal. From this and later experience I learned that a plain tea in Ireland really is a plain tea. No buns or cakes are served, as is usual in Britain, and in some places not even jam, nor did I ever see cress. Generally there are two kinds of bread, baker's and homemade, and English visitors sometimes call the latter soda bread, though I have not heard the term used by anyone Irish. The price was usually 1s 6d, sometimes 1s 9d, or even 2s, but occasionally (as at Lough Bray) only 1s 3d. The housewife here asked for an entry in the visitors book, possibly to convince the food office that she was entitled to all the tea, sugar and butter she claimed, but as two recent callers had signed themselves Dorothy and Lillian Gish of Hollywood, I am not sure of the book's value as evidence.

Behind the cottage and hidden from the road but only 100m away, lies Lower Lough Bray, one of two beautiful glacial lakes that nestle under a high granite promontory called Eagle's Crag. The upper lake lies in a higher col, hidden from view from the lower lake by a great moraine. The two lakes are often referred to simply as Lough Bray in old literature. The name dates back as far as 1580, when it appears as Lough Brai on Boazio's map of Ireland. One interpretation of the name is the Gaelic, Loch Breagh, or the Lake of the Hill. The earliest good description of them I have found is that of John Trotter, written in 1812:

> In a short time, however, we arrived at two beautiful small lakes, near the road, called Loughchree.[59] They were surrounded by mountains, and of a pellucid blue. Their shores were rocky, and their environs seemed the residence of peace and solitude! Not a habitation was to be seen! The Heath and moss spread a green carpet everywhere, and clothed the mountainsides in a charming manner, whilst a small shrub mixed its tender verdure here and there.[60] Not even the solitary king's-fisher, with rapid flight and short cry, broke the calm silence that reigned!

Black's Guide of 1879 refers to Upper Lough Bray as 'a dreary mountain tarn' while 'the lower lake is highly picturesque ... relieved by the beautiful rustic *cottage of Lough Bray*', a suggestion that for a place to be truly 'picturesque', it needs to have the mark of man.

Oliver St John Gogarty was a frequent visitor, and he wrote about a picnic on the nearby shores of Lough Bray in *As I Was Walking Down Sackville Street*:

> A hundred yards from the road by a path that borders a rivulet the edge of the lake is reached. An ancient crater makes three quarters of an amphitheatre which opens to the south and east. The lake lies deep within. Beyond, the semi-circular cup is dark green like the

---

59 Lough Bray.
60 The two lakes are named Upper and Lower Lough Bray, and the small shrub referred to is probably the Irish variant of the blueberry, the fraughan, which still grows thickly on the hillsides here. In early summer the fraughan puts out leaves of the palest green.

colour that invests Eternity. Pinewoods lie in a level to the right and hem a crescent of white sand.

By the granite outcrops the feast was spread. One of the rocks made a natural table with its flat top. Hampers were unpacked. Hard by, a cottage provided hot water for those who cared for tea. The sun shone on the lead-bright water....

We were on a high pleasant shelf. To see the valley it would be necessary to walk a hundred yards to the road: whence to the south east stood the peaks of the Golden Spears,[61] the Head of Bray, and beyond, a floor of shining sea. Some miles behind, a point might be reached from which Dublin could be seen smoke-veiled in its plain: St Patrick's Cathedral seemingly still its highest and greyest mass beneath a pall of smoke, though Christ Church is higher. The dear and fog-crowned Athens of my youth!...

The lake by which we lolled was a crater once. Our very table, tricked out with mica, was of igneous rock that told of old incredible cataclysms before man narrowed Time to be a measure of his years and superimposed his squabbles on the silver-shining granite that had reached eternal rest.

Although the lower lake is very close to the road, its hidden nature ensures that in other than high summer it is infrequently visited. From the ridge of the moraine between the two lakes a steep path leads up to the granite tor called the Eagle's Crag and a shelf that cantilevers spectacularly out over the lower lake. It is a wonderful viewpoint at any time of the year. In spite of the nuisance of marauding ravens, peregrines usually nest in the crags south or north of Eagle's Crag, and you can watch their young being trained to hunt during the late months of summer. Feral goats inhabit the cliff tops, and deer are often seen far below shading themselves in the mossy wilderness of gnarled old trees and great bushes of fraughans, heather and bracken at the southern end of the lower lake. The lakeside is always a great place for good, fat, juicy fraughans in late summer, and you will occasionally see serious harvesters there, usually of the older generation, bent over the low bushes, patiently filling containers with the little berries.

---

61   Probably Great and Little Sugarloafs

The Military Road winds up steeply from Lower Lough Bray until, in a higher, cliff-backed corrie, Upper Lough Bray comes into view over to the right. On the way the skew bridge built by Taylor's men is crossed. At the top of the hill you can stop and park in the old quarry; a path leads from the side of the road down to the upper lake and across the upper moraine to the lower lake.

LOUGH BRAY

Now Memory, false spendthrift memory,
Disloyal treasure, keeper of the soul,
This vision change shall never wring from thee,
nor wasteful years effacing as they roll
O steel blue lake, high cradled in the hills,
O sad waves filled with sobs and cries
White glistening shingle, hiss of mountains rills
and granite hearted walls blotting the skies;

Shine, sob, gleam gloom forever, Oh in me
Be what you are in nature – a recess –
To sadness dedicate and mystery
Withdrawn, afar in the soul's wilderness
Still let my thoughts leaving the worldly roar,
Like Pilgrims wander on thy haunted shore

STANDISH O'GRADY

The road now leaves the valley of Glencree and the two loughs behind as it winds out onto the high plateau east of Kippure, 500m above sea level, and ahead is a new skyline of the rounded summits of Carrigvore (682m), Gravale (718m) and Duff Hill (720m), like a series of great purple waves flowing southwards towards Wicklow's second highest mountain, Mullacleevaun (849m). To the right is the shallow dome of Kippure, topped by a television mast. The county boundary between Dublin and Wicklow crosses the summit of Kippure, which was chosen in 1960 as the best location for the television mast that would distribute the signal from Telefís Éireann, Ireland's first television station, to secondary distribution points on mountain summits around the country.

The late Oliver Flanagan, a Fine Gael TD, is said to have commented that before television there was no sex in Ireland, and there is no doubt that the medium was responsible for bringing the population of Ireland truly into the modern age. The advent of Irish television was at least partly attributable to the increasing ease with which transmissions from the BBC were being received in the Republic, and a Television Commission was set up in March 1958 to look into the matter of setting up a national television service. Enabling legislation was passed in 1960, and planning began shortly after.

While building works began in Montrose in Donnybrook in Dublin on the new studios, building was also taking place in very different conditions, at 757m above sea level, on the summit of Kippure.

The mast itself was built by Huso Werft, a Norwegian company whose speciality was enlarging ships by cutting them in half and adding a section in the middle.[62] Unfortunately, construction of the mast involved the destruction of the small prehistoric cairn on the summit. Wicklow County Council built the access road from the Military Road up to the transmitter buildings on the summit, and, used timber logs as the road base in areas of deep peat. As soon as the mast was erected, transmission tests began from the Telefís Éireann broadcasting station at Montrose, with signals transmitted by a high mast which was in line of sight of the top of the mast on Kippure. During early tests, there were mysterious brief interruptions in the signal received by the Kippure mast. Engineers worked through the night checking the equipment but could find no faults. The problem was eventually identified as a need to raise the transmitter a metre or two – the interruptions were caused by grazing sheep moving about on the mountain.

It was a remarkable achievement, long forgotten now, that from the passing of the enabling Broadcasting Act, it took a mere twenty months to have a complete television station up and running for its first broadcast on New Year's Eve 1961, when 300,000 people watched on 30,000 television sets.

---

62 *A Brief History of Television in Ireland*, Kevin J. O'Connell.

The summit of Kippure in 1914   Courtesy of Peter Healy

To the left of the road is a broad, high moorland called Powerscourt Mountain, which stretches from Enniskerry all the way to Kippure, and was formerly owned by the Lords Powerscourt. The two low summits which rise from this moorland are Tonduff (642m) and War Hill (686m), which rather than having something to do with fighting, is only an anglicised version of cnoc a' bharr, or the hill of the summit. Between these two hills the River Liffey rises, and the first of the many bridges over the river is that carrying the Military Road. In ancient times all this land belonged to the tribes of the territory of Cuala, until it came into the possession of the Norman family of de la Poer, connected by marriage to followers of Strongbow or Richard le Clare, who lead the Norman invasion of Ireland in 1169. In 1535 the lands were reclaimed by the Wicklow O'Toole clan, only to be retaken by the English and granted to the Talbots. Another great Wicklow/Wexford clan, the Kavanaghs, reclaimed them for the Irish in 1556, but they were finally lost to Richard Wingfield, who was granted them for putting down the rebellion of Cahir O'Doherty in the north of Ireland in 1608. In 1743 the Wingfield of the time became Viscount

The summit of Kippure today ⟶

Liffey Head Bridge 1915

Courtesy of Peter Healy

Powerscourt, and their ownership of a great area of mountain and valley lands, amounting to 21,000 acres in the mid 19th century, continued until the late 20th century.

Taylor reported in February 1802 that '5 miles forward on the direct road to Sally Gap and beyond it towards Seven Churches are nearly half finished'. This stretch between Glencree and the Sally Gap takes the Military Road to its highest point of 520m above sea level, just beyond the Liffey Bridge, and it can be a bleak place even in summertime.

138

The bridge constructed over the Liffey by Taylor's men is a particularly fine and robust structure, but after a hundred years there were some signs of collapse and a long buttress was built on the north east side, to give the retaining wall additional support. This intervention was reinforced rather crudely in the 1950s when two circular concrete pipes were placed under the bridge and surrounded with concrete. As they did in all their bridges, Taylor's masons floored the stream bottom, upstream and downstream of the bridge, with robust cobbles to prevent strong winter flows from undermining it, and these cobbles can still be seen in place today.

A twenty-minute walk through rough heather and moor grass, very wet and boggy in places, will take you to the source of the Liffey. About a kilometre from the road, and a little less in summertime, there are a number of dark peat-stained pools, some with a froth that resembles the head on a pint of Guinness. These hallowed waters appear from under the peat and disappear again a few times before a vigorous and continuous brook runs westwards towards the road, at the beginning of its long journey west and north and then eastwards through Dublin city and into the Bay. James Joyce wrote in *Finnegans Wake* that the Liffey begins 'on the spur of the hill in old Kippure, in birdsong and shearing time, but first of all, worst of all, the wiggly livvly, she sideslipped out by a gap...while Sally her nurse was sound asleep....'

St John Gogarty described it as

> ...gathering water from that many-fountained hill before it could risk a long journey without being foiled by the flatness of its moors. For sixty miles it would wind through the loveliest valleys in the world to Brittas by Kilbride, where the Shankill river rushes to meet it through a gorge of rhododendrons and oaks, then meandering, it will fall at Poulaphouca down to the level plain of Kildare... .

South of the infant Liffey, on a raised bank which stands higher than any other ground between War Hill and Kippure, are the remains of what is called on the Neville's 1756 map 'Ld Powerscourt's Game Keepers House', and is today more commonly known as 'The Grouse House'.

This building, which measured 6m by 4.5m, predates the Military Road by at least 50 years, and is the earliest known man-made structure in this upland area. The dimensions do not suggest that this was a hunting lodge of the scale of nearby Luggala or later, more elaborate post-Act of Union lodges, many survivors of which can be found around the country, where shooters or hunters were accommodated overnight in tight but luxurious ambiance. It seems that this building was a landmark where shooters might have assembled before and after a grouse shoot, having arrived there on horseback. Its prominent location would have allowed grouse shooters wander for hours in search of the birds with little danger of getting lost – even in its ruined state it is visible even from the Featherbeds. From it you can glimpse the Irish Sea and the tops of Sugarloaf, Mullacleevaun, Tonelagee and Scarr. What remained of its gable wall was a well-known landmark in a landscape with few landmarks for many years until it was blown down in a storm in January 2004. Within a month or two it was roughly re-erected by unknown persons, who clearly appreciated the navigation services it has been providing for so many years.

From its highest level after the crossing of the Liffey, Taylor took the road in almost a straight line for nearly a kilometre, one of the longest straight stretches in the entire road, gently dropping towards the Sally Gap, under Carrigvore. If you follow the road today there can be very little difference in what you see around you from the landscape in which Taylor's Fencibles laboured in the spring and summer of 1801. The television mast on Kippure and the scattered trees along the southern side of the moorland Liffey valley to the west are the only additions to the scene. The trees are what remain of the Coronation Plantation, an ill-fated attempt to afforest the upper Liffey area in 1831 by the Marquess of Downshire, who named the plantation to celebrate the coronation of the Sailor King, William IV. Today the uplands of the Wicklow and Dublin mountains usually consist of either one thing or the other, open expanses of treeless moorland or dense coniferous forests. The 4sq. km of the Coronation Plantation is neither, but a moor with a broad and picturesque scattering of pines, oaks, alders and rowan, resembling the African veldt at times in high summer.

Where the plantation, the Liffey and the road come together, a little more than a mile west of the Sally Gap, is an excellent place for a picnic. Nearby there is an obelisk erected by the Marquess of Downshire to commemorate the development of the plantation. The inscriptions can be difficult to read, but indicate that the trees were planted 'for a future supply of useful timber for the Estate and the improvement of the County and the Benefit of the Labouring Classes'.

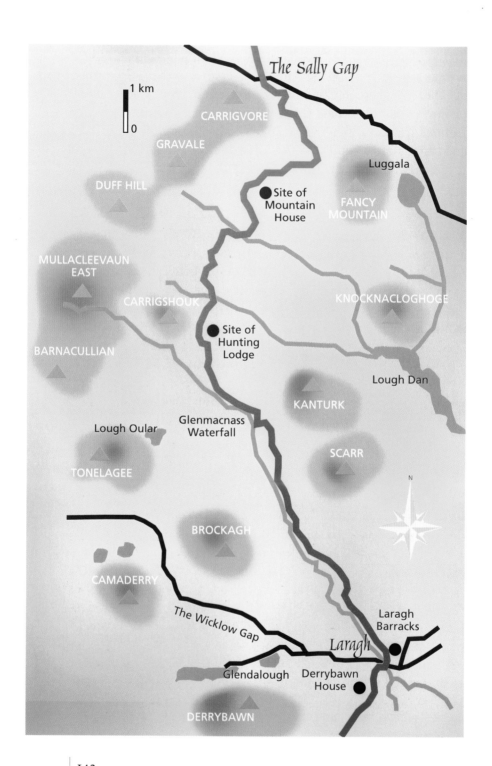

The Sally Gap

1 km

0

CARRIGVORE

GRAVALE

DUFF HILL

Luggala

FANCY
MOUNTAIN

● Site of
Mountain
House

MULLACLEEVAUN
EAST

CARRIGSHOUK

KNOCKNACLOGHOGE

● Site of
Hunting
Lodge

BARNACULLIAN

Lough Dan

KANTURK

Lough Oular

Glenmacnass
Waterfall

SCARR

TONELAGEE

N

BROCKAGH

CAMADERRY

The Wicklow Gap

Laragh
Barracks

Laragh

Glendalough

Derrybawn
House ●

DERRYBAWN

The Sally Gap to Laragh

8

The Sally Gap, at 500m above sea level, is one of two east-west passes through the Wicklow Mountains. There is no sense of there being an actual 'gap', and only from a distance to the west is it possible to see that there is a slight dip there between the rounded granite hills to the north and the south. It is very likely that the east-west route through the mountains via the gap has been used by man for thousands of years: east of the Sally Gap it is likely that the track followed the Cloghoge River down past Lough Tay to reach the coastal plain via Lough Dan. When the valley of Lough Tay was reclaimed and cultivated in the mid-18th century, the ancient track was probably diverted up along the east side of the valley, a high track that was called for some reason lost in the past 'The Murderin' Pass'.

When Taylor and his men reached the Sally Gap early in 1801, they would have met a bridal track, passable in summer but difficult in places in winter. It would have been the first trace of a mountain track they would have come across since leaving Glencree 3 miles to the north, and when they left it behind, they faced the longest single traverse of wilderness of the whole Military Road, over 7 miles of high empty moorland, to reach the head of the valley of Glenmacnass. The photograph overleaf shows the road at the Sally Gap as it was in 1914, a little over a hundred years after construction. Although with a gravel finish, and this photograph is taken in dry weather, the surface seems very good at this point and appears well used. We know from one of Taylor's reports (25 April 1809) that some years after being first constructed the road in this area had deteriorated, becoming 'flat and hollow in the centre', and had to be repaired.

The section of the Military Road from the Sally Gap to Laragh was

143

The Sally Gap 1914

closed during World War II, and grass grew over it. John Wood, on a walking tour around Ireland in 1947, wrote:

> Farther down were the crosstracks called the Sally Gap, amidst scenes as desolate as any that I saw later in the west, though I was never out of sight of diligent turf-cutters anxious for their winter fuel supply. Ahead was what the map called a military road – a relic of the British occupation. The first mile or two had been dressed with road metal for the benefit of the turf lorries, and this incidentally made it unfit for nailed boots like mine, but for the rest of its length it cannot have been mended much since the army built it in redcoat days. Grass along the middle was grateful and comforting, as the cocoa ads used to say, to feet tired with tarmac. If only the county council will refrain from 'improving' it further, the military road will remain

one of the finest ways for walkers in the land. Ups and downs are avoided by winding round at the 1,200 foot contour line, and thus are revealed from time to time fresh aspects of the powerful heights.

Before Taylor's men left the Sally Gap behind, however, there was some additional work to do. A little over 2 miles down the bridal track to the east towards Roundwood, nestling in the deep glacial Lough Tay valley, the La Touche family had a fine hunting lodge at Luggala. David La Touche was a banker with considerable political influence, and he persuaded the Lord Lieutenant to instruct Taylor to build a bridge where the bridal track crossed over the Cloghoge River by way of a ford. The bridge, which cost, according to Taylor's accounts, £70, was replaced early in the 20th century, but had to be built again when it was washed away during the onslaught of Hurricane Charlie in 1987.

The dramatic glacial landscape of the valley of Lough Tay, where the La Touche hunting lodge can still be seen today, is one of the most scenic places in Wicklow. It was described as follows in 1801[63] before the Military Road reached the Gap:

A very slender stream proceeds to Lough Tay, which forms a beautiful basin of about three miles in circumference, situated at the bottom of the most stupendous and craggy mountain, one of which presents a most formidable appearance of an inaccessible precipice. On the other side, it seems overhung by a bold and rugged mass, with mountains piled around. Passing from the Gap by a narrow defile, on the summit of this mountain, with the lough immediately below you, you are astonished at the perception in the bosom of this rugged crater, of a polished surface of the most verdant meads, interspersed with a variety of the leafy tribe. Curiosity is on the wing to form a conjecture of the friendly hand which has relieved with such delightful scenery, this forbidding waste. The enchantment is fully explained when you recognise, in opening on the view of Luggala, the hand of a Latouche.

In spite of the late date, this description has the pre-18th-century

---

63 *Mountains of Britain*, Edward Pyatt

attitude that all wildernesses and mountains in particular are essentially ugly and only the harnessing of nature by man produces 'scenery'. The account also indicates the perceived stature not only of David La Touche but the La Touche family; and as the description of Lough Tay valley could easily apply today, it is evidence of the state of agricultural development of the valley even at this early stage. The landscaping at Luggala was the work of Peter La Touche who, after creating a romantic landscape at his country seat at Bellvue, County Wicklow, bought the lands around Lough Tay as far south as Lough Dan about 1787 and built a gothic 'cottage mansion' style hunting lodge and laid out a rustic landscape around it. Hermann, Prince von Puckler-Muskau wrote of the place in 1828: 'It is indeed a lovely spot of earth, lonely and secluded, the wood full of game, the lake full of fish, and nature full of poetry.' At some time in the first half of the 19th century it was sold to the Wingfields, Viscounts Powerscourt, who in turn sold it in 1937 to the Guinnesses. Garech Browne of that family is still in residence. In 1956 the house burnt down, but it had been extensively recorded in photographs, and the architect Alan Hope was commissioned to rebuild it exactly as it was. During the years Garech Browne has lived here, many musicians, poets, writers, artists, actors and film-makers have visited Luggala, a very long and eclectic list which includes the pop star Mick Jagger, the traditional piper Leo Rowsome, the film-maker John Huston, the writer Patrick Kavanagh, and the poet Seamus Heaney.

The house is only glimpsed from the road above, and you either have to climb Fancy Mountain that rears above Lough Tay to the west or park along the road and make your way across the wall of the 'Murderin' Pass' and steeply down through the grassy hill to get a good view of it. Herds of deer often graze the lands between the house and the lake, and in one of the meadows stands a little domed and columned temple built from granite. It was originally erected at Templeogue House in south County Dublin in the 18th century by the Domville family, and when they moved to Santry Court in north County Dublin later in that century, they brought the little temple with them. When Santry Court was being demolished in the 1950s, the temple escaped destruction when it was moved again to the grounds of

Luggala House

Luggala. It was re-erected as a memorial to Tara Browne, brother of Garech Browne, who was tragically killed in a motor accident in 1966.

Indeed, other than improvements to the precipitous winding road that runs high over the valley, a road called in the old days 'The Murderin' Pass', little has changed about this area in the centuries

147

since the hunting lodge at Luggala was built, and it is a popular stopping place for passersby. When the walker J.B. Malone came upon the valley for the first time, walking from Rathfarnham in 1933, he wrote: 'Some things can be described: but Lough Tay, seen after marching through the high bogs of the Sally Gap, cannot be. If this is earth, then what is Heaven?'

From the Sally Gap the Military Road climbs gently to follow the contours below the rounded summits of Carrigvore, Gravale and Duff Hill. A new horizon opens up to the south and east, an endless parade of Wicklow tops stretching into the distance, and to the south-east in clear weather the Irish Sea glints beyond Wicklow Head.

Lord Hardwicke, appointed to take Charles Cornwallis's place as Lord Lieutenant, carried out a tour of inspection of the Military Road early in 1802, eighteen months after the work on the road had commenced, and requested a report on the project and its progress from Alexander Taylor. The reply, written in Taylor's exquisite hand and entitled 'Report of the present state of the Military Road now making thro the Mountains in the Counties of Dublin and Wicklow', was submitted on 10 February 1801.[64] The document stated that work on the road had extended south of the Sally Gap and that the project had so far cost £6,901, which included £70 for the construction of a bridge near Luggala at the request of Lord Cornwallis, £230 for the provision of the 'Soldiers Hutts' at Glencree, and £600 for bridges, sewers and water pavements. At this stage Taylor estimated the projected cost of the road as far as Aghavannagh as £20,300.

Lord Lieutenant Hardwicke must not have been entirely satisfied by Taylor's report, because on 22 April he had Chief Secretary Little-hales request the answers to a list of specific queries. In particular, Hardwicke wanted to know when the project might be finished, what arrangements were being used for engineering aspects of the work, such as the erection of bridges, and whether there was any possibility of local labour being used if the military had to be withdrawn. Clearly, although Michael Dwyer was still at large and causing some

---

64 Official Papers 293/1(11).

difficulties, there had been a considerable relaxation of the security situation by 1802. Regiments were being disbanded and soldiers were being sent home, and it is possible that Taylor had already lost many of the original two hundred soldiers he had started with. Hardwicke also alluded to the fact that there had been delays in the surveying of the southern section of the road, probably that from Laragh to Aghavannagh, qwing to Taylor's 'occasional absences', and wanted to know if it would be necessary to employ an assistant while Taylor was 'employed elsewhere'. It seems clear from this comment that the Lord Lieutenant was aware that Taylor was not solely involved with the Military Road, and had his fingers in other pies.

Indeed, Taylor did have a thriving private practice in surveying and map-making, for which he sometimes received leave of absence. Official Papers include a letter dated 20 November 1801 from Richard Lovell Edgeworth to the Under Secretary regarding the preparation of a 'statistical view of the County of Longford' for the Dublin Society. He says that the Captain Taylor of the Royal Engineers 'was employed some years since to make a map of this county which he has been prevented from finishing' because of to his Military Duty. He goes on to say that the previous Lord Lieutenant, Lord Cornwallis, had promised leave of absence for Taylor to finish the work, and as he was aware that Taylor had an opportunity at the moment (probably due to the winter conditions in the mountains) he asked if it would be possible that he could be released for a short period to do so.[65] In fact, Taylor had collaborated with Edgeworth and his son, William, in laying out the trigonometrical foundations for the survey, but it seems he was not released or chose not to go to Longford. The long-awaited map of the County of Longford was eventually published by William Edgeworth in 1814.

Taylor took only two days to provide answers to Hardwicke's queries. He reported that the completion date depended on the number of men he could obtain to work on the project, and adroitly put the matter back in Hardwicke's court by saying if he had two hundred soldiers and one hundred 'country labourers' the road could be finished as far as Laragh before the end of 1802 or early the following year. He

---

65 Official Papers 106/27.

went on to say that the North Cork Militia had already been withdrawn, but he hoped the Duke of York's Fencibles would remain, and that the Lord Lieutenant would send more troops to replace the Militia as soon as the weather improved. He also reported that he had been able to employ, on contract, farm labourers who lived local to the road, but found 'few of the country people in that neighbourhood who seem inclined to work, they come for a few days and go away again so often' and that they 'cannot be depended upon for any steady exertion they are not much accustomed to labour being mostly employed in herding cattle....' The largest number of labourers he had available to him at any one time was sixty, and this was when much of the work would have been in the area between Rathfarnham and Glencree, where there was an appreciable population.

It seems that delays in the construction of bridges and drains along the 9-mile stretch between the Sally Gap and Glenmacnass were holding up the completion of difficult sections of the road and, in turn, bridge-building materials could not be transported to site on an unfinished road. The small quarries which had been opened where granite was available along the route would have provided plenty of rough stone which, broken up into small cobbles, would have been used in the bed, in some places quite deep, of the road. Gravel for the surface dressing of the road may have been taken from the many streambeds that the road crossed, and broken up *in situ* with sledgehammers. But none of these way-side quarries, that can still be discerned along the Military Road, with the possible exception of the large quarry above Upper Lough Bray, produced granite of suitable quality for the large structural sections needed for bridges. Bridge materials, therefore, which included substantial single-piece lintels weighing not much less than two tons, had to come from granite quarries in the Rathfarnham/Edmond-stown/Killakee areas. They in turn could not be transported until the road to each bridge position was finished.

Taylor reported that initially it was the masons of the two detach-ments that had been provided to guard the work and the workers, the

---

66 T. F. Mills, Fencible Regiments of the British Army.

Luggala temple

Duke of York's Fencibles from Banffshire[66] and the North Cork Militia, that had carried out the bridge and sewer work, but subsequently this work had been carried out under contract using the original specifications.

With regard to the Lord Lieutenant's concern about Taylor's availability on the southern section of the road between Laragh and Aghavannagh, he reports that nothing had been done with regard to the survey of the 'southern district', which is through mountainous terrain, because he understood this section was not urgently wanted. He would, however, be ready to start it the 'moment it is desired', and that his assistant Lieutenant Mackintosh was fully capable of directing the work in his absence.

Around the time that Hardwicke carried out his inspection of the road, local landowners took the opportunity to propose to the Lord Lieutenant that the government might purchase land along the road south of the Sally Gap, in the very centre of the mountains, and settle disbanded soldiers from the Fencible regiment there to reclaim and develop the land. It was felt that these Protestant Scots would prove 'loyal' citizens who would be capable of reclaiming and improving the bog land, something that was being proposed generally in relation to the Irish bogs at the time. Subsequently, with the technology of the time, bog reclamation did not prove to be a viable option, particularly in such deep blanket bog areas. Hardwicke was favourable to the idea but this 'plantation' plan failed when difficulties arose about purchasing plots in lands that were in the ownership of the See of Dublin, which at the time was the second largest landowner in Wicklow.[67]

During this time Michael Dwyer and his men were still at large in Wicklow, but there is no record of any attempts being made to disrupt the work on the road, even though the route through which the road ran passed close to many recorded hideouts that were in use by the rebels at the time. The detachment of soldiers assigned to the project to protect the road workers would have helped in this regard. Often rebel hideouts were located close to the houses of loyalists, where

---

67 Land and Landscape in County Wicklow c. 1840, William Nolan, *Wicklow History and Society*, Geography Publications, 1994.

presumably the rebels were assured of a supply of food and intelligence from the servants of the house. One such hideout was known in a cave or cleft in the field of large boulders below the cliffs at Luggala, in which a dilapidated musket of the 1798 period was found in 1937.

When the short-lived Treaty of Amiens was signed between France and England in March 1802, Michael Dwyer is reported as having been almost reduced to despair. There are no records of any rebel activity from his group during the period of European peace that lasted until early in 1803. Dwyer himself moved about under cover between Dublin, Carlow, Wexford and Wicklow, during which time he took steps to stamp out faction fighting which, in the absence of more purposeful activity, had broken out again. It is said that he frequently visited the Yellow House Inn in Rathfarnham to meet Dublin dissidents. Michael Eades, the owner of the Yellow House, although a sergeant in the local Volunteers, was said to have sympathies with the United Irishmen, but (*see page 44*) may have played both sides. We know Dwyer was in the Coombe in Dublin in March 1803 taking part in discussions about a new uprising. This was to be staged in Dublin under the leadership of Robert Emmet, and at that meeting in the Coombe, although doubtful about the dependency of Emmet, Dwyer agreed to meet with him to plan how the Wicklowmen might play their part.

It was in Rathfarnham, a short distance from where the Military Road begins, that Dwyer's contribution to the forthcoming Dublin rebellion was plotted. Emmet had rented an isolated house in Butterfield Lane, a winding bohereen that connected Rathfarnham to Firhouse, where he planned to put the final touches to the plans for the rebellion. He knew Rathfarnham well: his brother Thomas Addison Emmet had had a villa there, close to the starting point of the Military Road at Rathfarnham Castle, and he was used to visiting his friend Richard Curran at The Priory, a mile to the south-east. He subsequently, in 1802, became romantically involved with Curran's sister, Sarah.

The meeting between the Wicklow men and Emmet took place in April 1803. Dwyer arrived at the house on horseback with a large group of companions. The conference went on for three days and Dwyer, characteristically nervous of betrayal and capture, never slept during the time and refused to allow anyone to leave the house. His constant caution had always paid off during his years on the run in Wicklow: the stories of his extraordinary escapes are still legends there. Egged on by Emmet, he undertook to provide a force of 5,000 men within two days of the beginning of the rising, but said he would not move until cannon were firing in Dublin. In return, he was promised arms and ammunition, and within a few days new muskets, powder and pike handles were supplied from Emmet's Dublin stores and carted, hidden in loads of lumber, to the Glen of Imaal by Bryan Devlin. It is very probable that the Military Road, being the most direct and suitable route, was used for at least part of the journey for these deliveries. As with many of Dwyer's activities, it seems that even transfers of arms were made under the noses of the military. Devlin's carts had to ford the River Slaney very near Leitrim Barracks in the Glen of Imaal, then under construction, and one of the carts, carrying kegs of gunpowder, was immersed in the river and the powder was soaked. It was taken to a nearby house, however, and dried in the sun on sheets stretched on planks.[68]

Dwyer may have been very optimistic in promising 5,000 men for the rebellion, and Emmet very naïve in believing him, although at all times it seems that Dwyer's true strength was far less than the legend he had become would have people believe. As it turned out, Dwyer did not have to bring his men down from the mountains to assist in the abortive rebellion. He waited at Rostyduff in the Glen of Imaal for word from Emmet, but neither of the two emissaries whom Emmet sent made it to the mountains, and by the time the news of the outbreak of fighting in Dublin had arrived in Wicklow, it was already too late and the rebellion was over. With the possibilities promised by Emmet's rebellion gone, and no sign of a new French invasion, Dwyer and his band returned to small-scale disruptive activities.

Although not directly referred to in any of the documentation, it is very likely that work on the high moorland reaches of the road was suspended during the worst of the winter weather. It is interesting to imagine how the troops would have entertained themselves during

---

68 *The Life of Michael Dwyer*, Charles Dickson, p. 235, Browne & Nolan, 1994.

those periods. Locals in Glencree talk of the establishment of a sheebeen at the roadside at the head of the valley (*see page 112*) and no doubt leave would have been given to allow the soldiers make their way down to Enniskerry or to Ballyboden for recreation in Bugler's inn or the Yellow House inn.

The stretch of the Military Road beyond the Sally Gap is certainly the most remote and exposed of the whole route. A little more than a mile beyond the Gap the view south opens up, a vast amphitheatre of rolling moorland surrounded by mountains. Dominating all is the rounded top of Tonelagee ending a string of summits running south from Carrigvore, while the rugged ridge of Scarr and Knockna-cloghoge encloses the moor on the east. While as far as Glencree there had been plenty of tracks and bridleways intersecting the route of the road and being utilised as part of the route, from Glencree onwards, but for the Sally Gap track crossing, there was nothing but high moorland with deep peat cover. From the Sally Gap Taylor took a route that descended gently along the contours of the line of hills, Carrigvore, Gravale and Duff Hill, running south-west from the gap. The logistics of getting the work done can only be surmised. The best progress would have been made in summertime, when the workers benefited from the long hours of daylight and the drier conditions. The remoteness from their original base at Glencree, however, must have begun to become a problem beyond the Sally Gap. Initially, soldiers and their escorts would have marched out to the works from their 'hutts' in Glencree, but as the works moved farther away from Glencree, it is likely that overnight encampments were established at the road head, with food supplied from Glencree, rather than march back the increasing distance to the base. While this might have been satisfactory in good weather, the nature of the bog surface would not have made it a comfortable experience in wet conditions.

In a sheltered position beside the road a little more than 2 miles south of the Sally Gap, near the banks of the Cloghoge Brook, the remains of an extensive area enclosed by the remains of stone walls can be clearly seen to this day. I have found no documents that deal with the minutiae of the period between April 1802 and April 1806, and therefore no reference to prove it, but I think it is reasonable to suppose that at nearly 6 miles from Glencree this is what remains of another semi-permanent camp for the soldiers working on the road. If a stone house or houses had been built at this spot, the remains would still be there: it is unlikely that the 'mining' of stones of ruined buildings that occurs elsewhere would have taken place here in such a remote place. It seems reasonable to suggest therefore that, other than the stone walled enclosure, the soldiers were accommodated here in either tents or huts of timber and sod construction. There is a possibility that it was here that the settlement of Scottish Fencibles, 'loyal citizens', was envisaged. Long after the military had departed, whatever shelter they left behind may have been appropriated: local tradition has it that there was a house of some kind here in the later 19th century called Mountain House, which acted as a staging post along the road. It is said to have been lived in by a family called Brady, and they kept a few sheep and some cattle. At the time of the construction of the Military Road, the lands a little further south of this place were owned by a Mr Brady of County Clare (*see page 160*).

After 1803, with barracks completed at Laragh, Drumgoff and Aghavannagh, overnight accommodation for Taylor's men was less of a problem, although in summertime he seems to have resorted to the use of tents: Arthur Wellesley's diary notes 'about 100 soldiers encamped' south of Drumgoff in July 1806.

Although there are few signs of man's occupation of this moorland, it has to be remembered that before the peat bog began to grow, the landscape was most likely heavily wooded. The frequency over the last century or two with which turf-cutters have found artefacts in featureless bogs suggest that there may have been considerable populations in these mountains. Less than 3km to the east there is evidence of a prehistoric settlement in the form of possible house sites in the valley between Knocknacloghogue and Luggala mountains, and on the lower eastern slopes of Luggala overlooking Lough Tay. In the latter location and further south, there are a number of ruins of later dwellings and considerable areas of lazybed tillage marks, suggesting continuous occupation of these sheltered lands for maybe thousands of years. Nearby is a 12m-diameter, stonewalled enclosure, called by local shepherds 'the round pen', which may have had earlier origins than a century or two.

Before the Military Road reaches the first plantation of modern forestry along this section, about 700m east of the bridge over the Inchavore stream that forms the north-east boundary of the forest and 100m south of the road, turf-cutters made a find in 1944. It was an oval piece of granite, rounded on one side, and flat and smooth-surfaced on the other with a cross inscribed on the flat side, located over a metre below the surface of the bog, and a similar dimension from the bog floor. Nearly a half metre long and half as wide, it has been suggested that the object is a saddle quern, a primitive type of table on which corn is ground by hand with another 'D'-shaped stone. Such quern stones usually date from the late Bronze Age; it makes one wonder what else the bog hides here. On the other hand, the location of the find would have been roughly on what was almost certainly an early east-west cross-mountain route, from the Liffey by way of the Lavarney Brook to the pass between Gravale and Duff Hill and down to the valley of the Inchavore stream to Lough Dan, so the quern might have been in transit and lost when fording a winter stream.

While the open moorland through which this section of the Military Road passes looks totally deserted, a large population of deer frequent the area. They are mainly a hybrid breed of red and sika deer, and are well camouflaged and all but invisible at a distance from the road. Another reason why they are rarely seen is because they tend to congregate in sheltered, grassy areas such as the shallow valleys of the many moorland brooks that run south-eastwards towards the Cloghoge River or Lough Dan, and one has to seek them out on foot for a sighting. The Irish mountain hare is also represented in this area, and again will only be spotted if one traverses the area on foot.

The construction of the barracks along the Military Road began in 1803, independent of Alexander Taylor's road project, and while there are no records of Michael Dwyer's men attempting to disrupt the construction of the Military Road, there are a number of stories about how they delayed the building of the barracks. Early in June 1803, John Mernagh, a close friend of Dwyer and one of the last of the Wicklow rebels to be captured, led a group of men at night to Leitrim Barracks, then under construction. One of the men, a Laurence Kennedy, reported later that the walls at the time had been raised to '25 or 30 feet', and the rebels set to using crowbars to reduce them, and in no time 'an immense quantity of the work was cast down'.[69] They certainly did do some damage, but Kennedy's story and rumours suggested a somewhat exaggerated amount of damage. Captain Myers, the Inspector of Yeomanry, reported to Chief Secretary Little-hales at Dublin Castle on 21 June 1803 that Dwyer and his companions had visited the construction works at the barracks on many occasions and held conversations with the contractor and workmen, assuring them that they would not be harmed. He went on to say that the recent mischief was caused because the workmen got drunk, began to fight and broke a window or a door, and the actual damage done would cost no more than a guinea. The truth of the matter probably lay between the two descriptions, but the propaganda value for Dwyer was considerable, the location of the event even translating to the barracks at Drumgoff, where the story was embroidered to Dwyer blowing much of it up with gunpowder.

The records of Dwyer's depredations are as scarce as the reports of his miraculous escapes are numerous. He had become the great bogey-man of the loyalists of the time and there seemed to be a kind of frenzy to capture him. The newspapers of the period constantly berated the government on the matter.

It must be a matter of astonishment that an active, powerful and vigilant Government could never succeed in exterminating these banditti from these mountains, however difficult and inaccessible they may at first sight appear. The rebel who is intimately acquainted with the topography of the place has his regular videts and scouts upon the *qui vive* in all the most advantageous points, who, on the appearance of alarm, or the approach of strangers, blow their whistles, which resound through the innumerable caverns, and are the signal for the muster of those hardy desperadoes. They are generally attended by the chief himself, or by his brother-in-law, of the name of Byrne, a determined fellow, in whom alone he places confidence. They are both great adepts at disguising their faces and

---

69   *The Life of Michael Dwyer*, Charles Dickson, p. 392, Browne & Nolan, 1994.

persons and are thought to make frequent visits to the metropolis.[70]

Evidence of Dwyer's near-involvement in Emmet's rebellion spurred on efforts to get him to surrender, and in November 1803 the Lord Lieutenant, Lord Hardwicke, sent a message to Dwyer promising him his life would be spared and he would suffer only transportation, but could bring his family with him. When Dwyer rejected the offer, an energetic campaign was embarked upon to capture him. A reward of £500 was offered for his capture, and many of his known friends and relations were rounded up, thus denying him the help and support he had enjoyed up until then. Soldiers were billeted in every cottage in Glenmalure, and as the winter turned particularly cold Dwyer and all but one of his inner circle decided to give themselves up on condition that they would be sent to America.

Dwyer finally handed himself up to William Hoare Hume in south Wicklow on 14 December 1803. With the exception of a few individuals in Dublin Castle, the government had always grossly overrated the importance of Dwyer, and believed that he was one of the central planners of Emmet's rebellion. It had been thought that even at this late stage he could call on 25,000 men in Wicklow to support an uprising or invasion by the French. During the interrogations of Dwyer after his surrender, however, he willingly 'told all', giving a detailed description of his escapades, and the numbers of men he had available to him at the various stages of his 'campaign': it was an enormous relief in government circles when it emerged through these interrogations that all that was left of his former 'army' was a raggle-taggle bunch of tired countrymen.

After some delay, Dwyer, like Holt before him, was transported to Australia, where his family joined him, and where he was allocated 100 acres of uncleared land adjacent to grants to his Wicklow comrades Hugh 'Vesty' Byrne, John Mernagh, Arthur Devlin and Martin Burke. Falling foul of the local governor, William Bligh, former captain of *The Bounty*, however, he spent two years exiled from his home before finally establishing himself in Cabramatta, New South Wales. Appointed

---

70 *Walker's Hibernian Magazine*, November 1803

constable of the Georges River district and active in the colony's Catholic community, he eventually increased his landholding to 610 acres. He was appointed chief constable of the Liverpool district in 1820 but was later dismissed for drunken conduct and mislaying important documents. In financial difficulties by 1822, Dwyer was eventually bankrupted and spent several weeks in debtors' prison, where he contracted dysentery and died on 23 August 1825.

Originally interred at Liverpool, his remains were reburied in the Devonshire Street cemetery, Sydney, in 1878 by his grandson John Dwyer, who was then dean of St Mary's Cathedral. In May 1898 the coincidence of the planned closure of the cemetery and centenary celebrations for the 1798 rebellion suggested the second re-interment of Dwyer and his wife in Waverley cemetery, where a substantial memorial was erected in 1900. The enormous crowds attending Dwyer's reburial and the subsequent unveiling of the monument, on which is inscribed the words 'The Wicklow Chief', testified to the great esteem in which Irish-Australians held him, in spite of his later financial difficulties. Dwyer had seven children and has numerous descendants throughout Australia.

Between the Sally Gap and Glenmacnass, the Military Road crossed seven streams that had to be bridged before reaching a precipitous granite outlier of Mullacleevaun called Carrigshouk. The area here is scattered with great granite erratics, through which it seems Taylor wove the road rather than trying to blast the great rocks. At the time of the building of the Military Road this area and the desolate lands east of Mullacleevaun were in the ownership of a Mr Brady of County Clare. The Military Road inspired him to erect a hunting lodge to the east of Carrigshouk, possibly as the first step in further development which never took place. The Ordnance Field Surveyors noted the building as follows in the 1840s:

> A neat House, property of Mr Brady with about 30 acres of pleasure ground. It is kept by a gamekeeper and let for the shooting season to gentlemen, for which purpose it was built convenient to the mountains.

The hunting lodge was later owned by the Downshire family. Today only sections of the lower walls of the hunting lodge remain, with fragments of slates from its roof, under a cloak of moss. Of the pleasure grounds, nothing remains, the only characteristics marking out the place as different from its heathy surroundings are a plantation of Scots pines and a rich outcrop of fraughan bushes. An adjacent barn or outhouse, however, was extant up until the early 1970s. A local sheep farmer[71] told me that Republican forces used the barn during the Civil War as a hideout, and that in the 1970s the IRA used to use the wood below Carrigshouk for testing explosives, and hid materials in the rocks of the east face of the hill. It was they that finally destroyed the barn, he told me, apparently in a final explosives test.

From Carrigshouk the road climbs again onto the bog of Laragh West, scattered with great erratics. The proximity of this bog to Glenmacnass ensured that when the Military Road was completed much of the peat cover was harvested, and tree roots exposed in this work are plentiful evidence that this place was a forest before the bog developed.

Dominating the scene ahead now is the rounded dome of Tonelagee, Wicklow's third highest summit. On the north shoulder of the mountain, a short distance from the cliffs overlooking a glacial lake called Lough Ouler, an unusual cross-inscribed slab can be found. It stands beside what is today a well-used hill walkers' route between Mullacleevaun and Tonelagee, and what was probably in the far and distant past a trade and pilgrim route. Not much more than a metre high and facing east and west, each eroded face has a cross inscribed upon it, the design of which, with expanded terminals, suggests to some archaeologists that it dates from the 7th to the 9th century.[72]

Local people have suggested that it marks the boundary between three townlands, but there is also reason to believe that it marked a high pilgrim route to Glendalough from the north-west. The well-known St Kevin's road, an ancient paved pilgrim route from the west through the Wicklow Gap to Glendalough, was marked by a number

71 Tommy Healy, in an interview in July 2006.
72 Conleth Manning, *Wicklow Archaeology and History*, Volume 1, p. 28.

Cross-inscribed stone

of such cross-inscribed stones, some extant, although, with the exception of one at Glendalough near the Priest's House, similar cross designs to the Tonelagee cross are found only in Donegal and Kerry.

At Laragh West the Military Road descended gently to follow the east bank of the Glenmacnass River, and by this time the lowlands of south Wicklow would have been in sight for the labouring soldiers. Before reaching those lowlands, however, another major work of engineering had to be achieved.

Laragh West, with Tonelagee on the left

At the head of Glenmacnass Valley the Glenmacnass River plunges 80m down inclined shelves of granite to the flat green fields below. Here blasting was required to create a level bed for the road as it swung east within metres of the top of the waterfall, and then south again, down a 600m-long retaining walled ramp along the east side of the valley towards Laragh.

The fertility of Glenmacnass Valley would have ensured that it was inhabited from early centuries, and in the woods above the lower part of the valley, at Brockagh, the remains of small stone-built farmsteads can still be found, many of which may have been extant in the early 19th century. Six years after the road reached the valley, John Trotter described it, noting that 'small farmhouses, encircled with trees, here and there enlivened it' and it seems probably that the Military Road descending into the valley met with a pre-existing rural track which ran from Laragh as far as the head of the valley.

A new army commander, Lieutenant General Lord Cathcart, gave renewed impetus to the Military Road project when he resumed funding for it in September 1803, only a few weeks after the end of the abortive rising of that year. After Dwyer's surrender in December, however, there was another slow-down in the Military Road project, this time it seems for a long duration: Taylor appears to have lost all his contingent of soldiers some time early in 1804.[73] He found that he could not rely on getting sufficient civilian labourers and the section of road between the Sally Gap and Laragh, which included substantial works at the Glenmacnass waterfall, took the best part of four years to build.

There is a gap in the Dublin Castle documentation relating to the road from September 1803 until April 1806: however, the work and funding did continue on and off during the period. Between August 1800 and December 1807 the cost of the road averaged out at approximately £5,500 per year, but the annual cost was steadily increasing. The cost in 1801 was about £4,500, between December 1803 and December 1804 it had risen to nearly £6,500, and between December 1804 and December 1805 was over £7,500. However, as far as can be ascertained from the documentation available, the Military Road was completed as far as the village of Laragh by early 1806.

---

73 Letter from Taylor to Littlehales, 4 April 1806 (Official Papers 293/1 (12)).

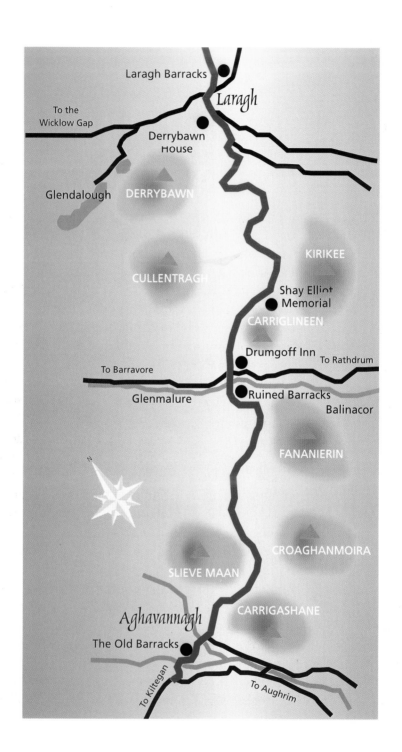

Laragh Barracks

Laragh

To the
Wicklow Gap

Derrybawn
House

Glendalough

DERRYBAWN

KIRIKEE

CULLENTRAGH

Shay Elliot
Memorial

CARRIGLINEEN

Drumgoff Inn

To Rathdrum

To Barravore

Glenmalure

Ruined Barracks

Balinacor

FANANIERIN

N

CROAGHANMOIRA

SLIEVE MAAN

CARRIGASHANE

Aghavannagh

The Old Barracks

To Kiltegan

To Aughrim

Laragh to Aghavannagh 9

At Laragh the Military Road meets with the R755 Roundwood to Rathdrum road, a road that predated it. At the time of the building of the Military Road, what is now the village of Laragh hardly existed as other than a junction that connected the main Roundwood to Rathdrum road with Glendalough, then known as The Seven Churches. The construction of the Military Barracks near the junction in 1803, followed by the arrival of the Military Road in 1806, made the place considerably more important and provided the impetus for the development of a village.

On the left of the road just before the village is the early 19th-century National School, now a private residence. Up a side road beside the old National School what remains of the barracks built at Laragh c.1803 can be found. With the exception of the granite window surrounds and the arched ground floor windows, it little resembles what it once was, although it has a tower to the left of the front elevation, a feature found only here and at Aghavannagh. It is thought that it was taken over as a constabulary barracks sometime after the military vacated it in the 1820s. A new constabulary barracks was built on the main road around 1840, after which the military barracks became disused again.

The Mining Company of Ireland was established in the Glendalough-Glendasan area in 1824 when it acquired the Luganure galena mine in Glendasan. Mining was probably the first industry to be practically assisted by the existence of the Military Road, as most of the ore from Glendalough and Glendasan, in the early days, had to be transported by mule-train to Ballycorus in County Dublin for smelting. They opened more exploratory shafts in the top of Glendalough Valley in 1850, and one shaft ran all the way through Camaderry mountain to Glendasan. Local tradition has it that the mining Company acquired the disused military barracks around that time and converted it into a residence by reducing it to two storeys, the length to seven bays, and topping the whole with corbelled castellations. It is thought that it was for a while the residence of the doctor appointed to look after the mine workers, and was later occupied by a member of the Parnell family. The mines used the converted barracks as a residence.

In spite of its imposing appearance, the accommodation is limited and the rooms are small. On the ground floor there is a kitchen, a sitting room and two other rooms; on the first floor a large bedroom and two smaller bedrooms, and a small room in the tower.

In 1928 Laragh Castle, as it had come to be known, was purchased by Maud Gonne McBride for Iseult, the daughter she had with the French politician Lucien Millevoye, and Iseult's husband, Francis Stuart. Iseult had followed her mother's footsteps as a 'modern woman', was briefly the mistress of the American writer Ezra Pound and was even proposed to by her mother's great admirer, William Butler Yeats, before meeting and marrying the young Francis in 1920. They moved into Laragh Castle in 1929 after restoration work had been carried out by Forans, well-known Dublin building contractors.

Francis Stuart (1902–2000) was a remarkable man whose literary career almost spanned the entire 20th century. Born in Australia of Irish parents, he was brought up in Dublin before attending boarding school in England. He wanted to be a poet, and from a young age he frequented the literary and artistic scene in Dublin, during the course of which he met Iseult. Through his mother-in-law, Maud Gonne, Stuart became involved with the Republican side during the Civil War, transporting guns and ammunition for them. Captured by Free State troops, he was jailed in Mountjoy and the Curragh, where he took the opportunity to read and write poetry. On his release in November 1923, he published his first book of poetry, which drew praise from Yeats.

At Laragh he enjoyed a fruitful period writing, at the same time earning a living through running a poultry business. He had considerable success at poultry breeding and was awarded a silver medal for the Department of Agriculture's competition 'for the Pullet non-sitting breed having the highest winter record of First Grade Eggs'.[74] In 1932 he published two novels, *Pigeon Irish* and *The Coloured Dome*, which were well received and sold very well.

Yeats came to visit the Stuarts at Laragh in June of the same year, but he stayed in nearby Glendalough in the Royal Hotel rather than Laragh Castle because he thought he would 'bore them and talk himself stupid'. While in Glendalough he wrote the poem, 'Stream and Sun at Glendalough':

> Through intricate motions ran
> Stream and gliding sun
> And all my heart seemed gay:
> Some stupid thing I had done
> Made my attention stray.
>
> Repentance keeps my heart impure;
> But what am I that dare
> Fancy that I can
> Better conduct myself or have more
> Sense than a common man?...

During the next seven years Stuart produced nine more novels, a volume of autobiography, and a horseracing book called *Racing for Profit and Pleasure in Ireland and elsewhere*, but none were as popular as his early work. In 1939 he was offered and accepted a post at Berlin University as a lecturer in English. He was on a visit home to see his family in September 1939 when the war broke out. He decided to return to his work in Berlin, however, and finding his way by a roundabout route, remained there for the rest of the war.

It was at Laragh Castle that the German spy, Hermann Goertz, stayed for a few days after his long trek from County Meath in 1940, (*see page 117*) during which it is said that Iseult fell in love with him.

---

74 *Manna in the Morning*, Madeleine Stuart p.108, Raven Arts Press, 1984 and *Francis Stuart – A Life*, Geoffrey Elborn, p.83 Raven Arts Press, 1990.

Laragh Castle today

Meanwhile in Germany Francis Stuart became involved in writing broadcasts for Berlin radio, and had an affair with Madeleine Gertrude Meissner, one of his ex-students. As the war progressed, conditions in Berlin worsened as bombing increased. By early 1945 the English department of the university where he worked had been destroyed, and with no job to keep him there, Stuart had the opportunity to escape from Berlin. He took Madeleine south to Munich and then to Bregenz, hoping to cross into Switzerland, but they were arrested by the Allies in November 1945, and held without charge on suspicion of spying. Stuart, however, escaped the fate of that other better-known Irishman, William Joyce, and was released in 1946. He and Madeleine lived for three years in Freiburg, where he wrote two of his finest novels, *Redemption* and *The Pillar of Cloud*. After a stay in Paris, the couple made it to London in 1951, where, after the death of Iseult Stuart in 1954, they married.

Iseult Stuart had remained in Laragh Castle during those years and was joined in 1951 by her sculptor son Ian and his German-born wife, Imogen, also a sculptor. Of the two, perhaps Imogen has become the best known in Ireland; working on church and public commissions, she has produced a very large corpus of work. Much of her work is in bronze and wood, and essentially Celtic in character, but it is enriched by her native expressionism and the carving traditions learnt as a student in Germany.

Imogen described Laragh Castle, when they lived there, as very primitive and damp, and all the water they used had to be hand-pumped. Maud Gonne McBride, then a very old lady, used to come to visit until she died in 1953: Iseult herself died a year later. Francis Stuart's mother Lily came to stay next, and she was there to greet Francis and his German wife when they eventually returned to Ireland in 1955. The Stuarts sold Laragh Castle in 1961: it was bought by the O'Kelly family, a member of which still lives there.

Below Laragh Castle in the trees is St John's Church of Ireland church, a simple structure of rubble stone, possibly from the demolished section of the barracks nearby. It was dedicated in 1867, after a long period of trying to collect sufficient subscriptions and a stop-go building period that began in 1843. It was built as a chapel of ease or a chapel of convenience of Derrylossery near Roundwood, to serve parishioners in the immediate vicinity of Laragh who might otherwise not attend services. Subscriptions towards the cost of the building were collected from local people and landowners, and included £15 from Her Gracious Majesty Adelaide, Queen Dowager. The nearby Catholic church of St Kevin, a larger and far more elaborate structure of cut stone, was commenced in 1847 and completed in 1851, indicating the ascendancy nature of the Catholic church at the time.

The village of Laragh is picturesquely surrounded by hills at the meeting point of four valleys, three rivers and three roads. When Taylor's Military Road construction crew arrived here, the new barracks was not long completed, and there was little else but a water mill, the cottages of the mill workers, and a humpback bridge taking the Roundwood to Rathdrum road over the Glenmacnass River. The landowner of the surrounding area at the time was a Captain Hugo, who owned one of the largest single holdings in Wicklow, but he sold his lands at Laragh and Annamoe to T. J. Barton in the 1830s. The new owner, grandfather of Robert C. Barton, Minister for Agriculture in the First Dail, was an 'improving landlord' and he set about improvements in the village: by the middle of the 1800s, Laragh was a thriving place.

The road leading west out of Laragh bifurcates a mile from the village, the northern fork climbing the Vale of Glendasan to the Wicklow Gap and on towards County Kildare, and the left fork leading into the dramatic, wild and romantic valley of Glendalough, known in 1800 as The Seven Churches. It got its name from the churches of that number scattered along the valley, built at, in or near the original monastic city that grew up from the settlement founded by St Kevin in the late 5th century. At the end of the 1800s the ruins of another church were found, and there is a further church mentioned in the annals, that of the Two Seneschals, that has as yet not been rediscovered, so this place might really have been called The Nine Churches. St Kevin, who died around 618 at the biblical age of 120 years, was from a Wicklow family of royal blood, and it is said that after considering Luggala further north for the site of his monastic settlement, he decided instead upon this long and deep valley with its two lakes. It is likely that the original monastery was sited in the area where the cathedral and round tower now stand. Tradition has it that the saint was buried under what is called the Priest's House today, a small building with Romanesque features and a slit window that may have been to allow the pilgrims to look inside the building at St Kevin's grave: more intimate access would have led to the wholesale removal of any loose stones and all the earth within the building, as happened to St Declan's burial place in Ardmore. However, St Kevin's Kitchen, a nearby building with a little round tower on its west gable, is roofed with a stone vault and may well have been where St Kevin's relics were kept and displayed: similar stone vaulted buildings at other monastic settlements such as St Flannan's Church at Killaloe, County Clare and St Colmcille's House at Kells, County Meath are thought to have been built to protect the relics of saints. St Kevin's Kitchen is the only building in Glendalough to survive almost intact for a thousand years, so the designer knew what he was doing.

Although Glendalough was abandoned around 1500, it continued to function as an important centre for pilgrims, and became one of the four chief places of pilgrimage in Ireland: the Latin Life of St Kevin states that seven pilgrimages to Glendalough are the equivalent to one pilgrimage to Rome. Joseph Peacock's fine oil painting of 1817, now in the Ulster Museum, captures the scene of the pattern or saints day festival very well. The painting portrays not just a place of prayer, but a kind of holiday camp, a summer fair, a sports day for the hard-working peasantry, with the pilgrims dressed in their best clothes, taking part in games of cards or feats of strength or queueing at stalls selling food and drink. As time went on, however, the great gatherings in the complex of ruined churches for prayer and penance on the saint's day on the site had descended into drunken riots by the mid-19th century.

Sir William Wilde's description of the activities of the poor benighted Irish peasantry on pattern day leaves little to the imagination:

> ...an immense crowd usually had bivouacked, or were putting up tents or booths, or cooking their evening meal, gipsy-wise, throughout the space of the sacred enclosure. As soon as daylight dawned, the tumbling torrent over the rocks and stones of the Glendassan river to the north of 'The Churches' became crowded with penitents wading, walking or kneeling up 'St Kevin's Keeve', many of them holding little children in their arms....

Towards evening the fun became 'fast and furious'; the pilgrimages ceased, the dancing was arrested, the pipers and fiddlers escaped to places of security, the keepers of tents and booths looked to their gear. The crowd thickened, the brandishing of sticks, the 'hoshings' and

Glendalough

'wheelings' and 'hieings' for their respective parties showed that a faction fight was about to commence among the tombstones and monuments, and all religious observances, even refreshments, were at an end... .

One year, as many as a hundred policemen had to be brought in to quell the riots, and eventually the pattern was banned by the church.

At the dawn of the age of tourism in the mid-18th century Glendalough became one of the places travellers in Ireland wanted to visit, and these tourists in turn attracted beggars and entrepreneurial guides. A description of one of the latter is given in the *Dublin Penny Journal* of 1833:

A Glendalough Guide
c.1830, *Dublin Penny Journal*

Leaving my horse at a wretched inn near the bridge, I was accosted as I proceeded towards the churches, by a queer-looking fellow, attired in what was once a military frock coat, that might have been scarlet, but now by some dirty dye have assumed the hue of bog-water; this hung in stripes about his heels, with an old shapeless felt hat on his head, such as country boys call a cobbeen – his countenance was not less uncouth than his attire – a leering cautious cunning in the wink of his eye, a hooked miserly formed nose, a huge mouth, whose under lip hung loose and pendulous. The expression of the whole outward man denoted practised confidence, cunning and meanness. And of course, fact in their presentations was liberally drowned in outlandish fiction, plucking historical personages out of their true place in history and putting them interacting with mythical characters, all the time laced with what the English call Blarney, or 'a way of saying it': phrases like 'St Kevin learned Latin as fast as another would sup milk' or 'I'll tell you with all the veins of my heart sir.'

Glendalough remains today one of Ireland's most popular tourist attractions and its qualities are well covered in literature.

Early in 1806 pressure to get the Wicklow Military Road completed was increased again as the war with France became more desperate. Despite the victory of the British navy in the Battle of Trafalgar late in 1805, the great English hero Nelson was lost in that battle, and before the end of the year Pitt, the Prime Minister, had also died. Meanwhile Napoleon, now a self-declared Emperor, marched from strength to strength in continental Europe, with all opposition fading away, and Britain was on her own once again. The English Channel and the navy, however, continued to protect Britain from the march of French armies, but as an island nation she relied on sea-borne trade. Napoleon sought to starve the British by decreeing that no country should trade with Britain or her colonies, and Britain replied by using her strong navy to blockade France.

Following a request from Chief Secretary Littlehales, in April 1806 Taylor produced his first report for Lord Lieutenant Hardwicke on the progress of the road in nearly four years. He indicated that the road could be finished that year if he had his military contingent of workers restored to him, it had cost £39,000 to date, and would cost a further £4,850 to complete the last 4 miles to Aghavannagh. Following the submission of this report, Taylor received a new contingent of soldiers and funding, and progress on the road speeded up again.

In July 1806, Sir Arthur Wellesley, the future Duke of Wellington, carried out an inspection tour of some of the defences of the south coast of Ireland in the company of his brother William. On their way south from Dublin, probably at the request of Dublin Castle, they inspected the Military Road and its barracks. After breakfasting at Glencree Barracks with the Barrack Master, Captain Barry, and Major Taylor, they proceeded with Taylor to Laragh Barracks, which Wellesley remarked was exactly the same as that at Glencree. Leaving their carriage and horses at Laragh, they walked west along the road to Glendalough, which Wellesley found 'a curious place' with 'romantic scenery', and on returning headed for the Barracks at Glenmalure. He commented that the Military Road to Glenmalure was not yet laid (presumably he meant it was not finished) and was 'very bad', but that in spite of this section not being completed, he found that work was proceeding southwards from Drumgoff, where he 'walked about a mile up the mountain where there were about 100 soldiers encamped who are employed making the road and who are paid by piece work'. The party then returned to Drumgoff, where Major Taylor must have bade them farewell as they made for Rathdrum on a 'very bad road'.[75]

At Laragh the Military Road met and followed the old road south from Roundwood to Rathdrum. In Taylor's original plan for the route, after crossing existing bridges over the Glenmacnass and the Glendasan rivers at Laragh, the Military Road would cut off to the south, rising up into the mountains again along the eastern flanks of Derrybawn heading for Glenmalure.

While work on the Laragh to Drumgoff section was under way before the end of 1806, as mentioned by Wellesley, the section between Laragh and Drumgoff was still not laid at that time. The landowner of much of the lands the road would have to traverse, a Mr James Critchley of Derrybawn House just south of Laragh, was more concerned about the quality of the road and bridge on his land than he was worried about being burnt out again as he had been by rebels under General Holt during the rebellion. He refused to allow the work to proceed over his land until a county presentment was obtained giving the army possession. Having been so adversely affected during the rebellion, Critchley would have been a supporter of the Military Road idea, so one can only surmise he was either interested in the financial compensation he might obtain from the deal if and when the Grand Jury were to take over the road and make it officially a public road, or he did not trust Taylor, or both.

Just beyond the village of Laragh, in on the right, is the demesne of Derrybawn House. Some of the out offices have been converted into a retail woollen mill and souvenir shop, and you can follow the original road across a picturesque humpback bridge to reach them. South of the humpback bridge is Derrybawn House, the present fine house built in the early 1800s, the original having been burnt during the 1798

---

75 Arthur Wellesley's diary of his tour of defences in Ireland: NLI MS 4707.

The old Military Road bridge at Derrybawn

rebellion. The old road used to pass in front of the house, but in 1834 a new line of road was taken further east and a new bridge built (Bookey's Bridge, named after the landlord at the time) to keep the road at a greater remove from the house.

Beyond Bookey's Bridge the Military Road bears right and uphill through woodland, the beginning of a steady winding climb of 170m to a pass between Cullentragh and Kirikee mountains. There are a few dwellings along the way as this road climbs, and in spite of the good road and the agricultural cultivation evident for the first mile or two there is a distinct feeling that one is returning to the wilderness again.

When the road reaches a pass at 350m above sea level, this feeling is confirmed: a new horizon is revealed ahead across the heath, a series of mountain summits, including that of Lugnaquilla, the highest mountain in Ireland outside of County Kerry.

Near the pass there is a monument on the left side of the road to the competitive international cyclist, Shay Elliot, who made a significant contribution to Irish and world cycling. He used to train on these hills, and it is said that he tied a bag of cement to his cycle to give himself an additional challenge. Elliot was the first Irishman in almost one hundred years to make inroads into European cycling, and in 1963 was the first Irishman to wear the yellow jersey in the Tour de France, paving the way for riders like Seán Kelly and Stephen Roche. In retirement he made plans to organise an Irish international cycling team, but a failed marriage, the death of his son in an accident ,and financial problems became too much for him, and he took his own life in 1971.

The Military Road now descends between heather-covered hills into the valley of Glenmalure.

Although there had been a garrison in Drumgoff Barracks for more than two years, the arrival of the Military Road in the deep glacial valley of Glenmalure, the refuge for so many centuries of the rebellious Irish, must have been a significant moment for Taylor and all those involved in the project. The barracks had been built on the south side of the Avonbeg River, and was cut off in the wet season from the northern part of the valley. Here a large bridge of a quality and design not previously seen in conjunction with the Military Road was built, probably by contract, bringing the road to the south bank. It still stands today with two arched stonework spans of more than 5m each and a slender central pier. All the previous bridges were fine examples of functionality, but here there are decorative pilaster-like columnar additions to the central pier and the wing walls, and the superstructure of rough stone, with the exception of the copings, is stucco-rendered. The bases of the piers are constructed from finely cut granite blocks. The pilaster feature occurred also in the bridge further to the south across the River Ow which was demolished in 1907, and can also be found at the end of the Military Road in the bridge over the Aghavannagh River near the barracks of the same name.

The gateway to Glenmalure

All three of these bridges cost £500 each. There are two further bridges of the same 'pilastered' design west of Aghavannagh carrying 'Hume's Road' across streams at Slieveamough and Knocknagree, well past the end of the Military Road: these may well have been privately carried out by the same contractors for William Hoare Hume. Drumgoff Bridge is clearly visible in Petrie's watercolour of Glenmalure dated about 1820, in an age when every bush and shrub was harvested for fuel: today the bridge is cloaked with trees and shrubs and not easily viewed from afar.

Glenmalure is one of Ireland's finest examples of a glacial valley, and has the typical textbook 'U' shape. It extends 15km southeastwards towards Rathdrum from Table Mountain, 6km north of

Drumgoff
Bridge

Lugnaquilla. The floor of the valley, by virtue of the protection provided by the mountains north and south and the glacial soils with which it is carpeted, is very fertile and in spite of its remoteness has been successfully farmed for many centuries. The earliest known evidence of occupation of the glen is an oval-shaped platform 2 miles north-west of Drumgoff, thought to be the site of an early church.

Until the Military Road was built across the last wildernesses of Wicklow in 1809 to reach Glenmalure, the valley had but two possible approaches, a road from the east from Rathdrum, and a bridal track, only easily passable in summertime, from the west across the top of Table Mountain from the Glen of Imaal. For centuries Balinacor, at the southeastern end of the valley, had been the eyrie of the leaders of the most powerful Wicklow clan, the O'Byrnes, the best known of whom was probably Fiach McHugh O'Byrne. He was in his prime towards the end of the 16th century when Elizabeth I was on the throne. Gaelic manners, customs and dress were still the norm in O'Byrne's Wicklow, right under the noses and a thorn in the sides of the colonisers of the Pale. While most other Irish chieftains of stature had vowed allegiance to the crown by the 16th century and built English-style tower houses as their headquarters, O'Byrne, partly because of the remoteness and therefore safety of Glenmalure, and partly because of his clinging to the old ways, resided in a traditional pre-Norman Gaelic complex. An earthen rampart 32m in diameter, probably topped with a defensive, densely braided hedge of blackthorn, surrounded a main house and outhouses of timber construction. While all traces of the timber structures and the defensive hedge are long gone, the rampart survives on the hillside 700m south-west of the hamlet of Greenan.

It was Fiach McHugh, supported by James Eustace, Viscount of Baltinglass, who inflicted one of the rare defeats of an English army by Irish forces, in the valley in 1580. The newly appointed Lord Deputy of Ireland, Lord Grey de Wilton, resolved to put an end to the rebellion of O'Byrne and Baltinglass: with no north-south route through the mountains from Dublin that could take an army, de Grey decided to march his forces out into Kildare as if heading south, and then to turn abruptly east from Donard to cross Table Mountain into the valley of Glenmalure in a surprise attack. His officers, experienced in the wars in Ireland and obviously wary of Wicklow terrain as an ideal battle-ground, tried to warn the new Lord Deputy of the folly of his strategy, but to no avail. It was the month of August, and by the time the English forces had come over Table Mountain and were descending to the stony-floored valley, they were probably already tiring and not in the best condition for battle. The rebel Irish, however, who had been well warned of the English feint, were prepared and in wait, having disposed themselves on the steep and high flanks of the valley as the English marched wearily into the classic ambush.

It is said that de Grey's secretary on the day was Edmund Spenser and that one of the young officers in the force was Walter Raleigh. It is likely that the Irish had at least some early firearms, possibly arquebusses, because there are reports of O'Byrne taking the lead roof off the church at Crumlin south of Dublin on an earlier occasion during a raid on the Pale, for the manufacture of shot. When the Irish opened fire, some of the English turned to climb to get to their attackers, while others turned tail. The Irish then descended from the heights, wielding their great swords and slaughtered as many as eight hundred of the enemy, while the rest retreated in disarray, among them de Grey, who had to leave behind his caravan of possessions and clothes.

This ignominious beginning to his tenure as Lord Deputy was surely partly responsible for the uncompromising results of his next warlike encounter in Ireland. When he returned to Dublin from Glenmalure with much of his army weary but intact, he received news of the arrival of a Spanish expeditionary force on the coast of County Kerry to support the Munster Irish. After augmenting his forces, the Lord Deputy marched south, and arriving in Kerry at the beginning of November, laid siege to the earthen fortress of Dun an Oir. After a short time the six hundred Spanish and fifty of their Irish allies surrendered. Having laid down their arms expecting mercy, the Spaniards were all put to the sword and the Irish were hanged.

Fiach McHugh O'Byrne continued to harass the English, but they succeeded in getting close enough to burn his house at Balinacor in 1581. It was probably rebuilt, as O'Byrne is recorded as having been living there again a year later.[76] By January 1595, however, Fiach McHugh O'Byrne had been ousted from his headquarters by Lord Deputy Russell, who then proceeded to refortify the place and establish an English garrison there. O'Byrne returned before long and drove out the English garrison but in May 1597, by now an old man, he was caught unawares by an English force with only a few men to guard him, and was killed near his home. His pickled head was sent to Queen Elizabeth. His son Phelim continued resistance for a few years but eventually gave in to the Crown and, although O'Byrne's descendants continued in various ways to fight against English rule, Gaelic Wicklow died with Fiach McHugh.

Eventually the lands of Balinacor, which amounted to 8,179 acres by

---

76 *Wicklow, History and Society*, p. 244, Geography Publications, 1994.

1838, were taken over and developed by the Kemmis family, who created a fine demesne and deer park on the good land north-west of Greenane and south of the Avonbeg River, which descends here in a series of picturesque cascades and pools. They built a house there in the late 18th century, which was much added to in the 19th, additions that included an Italianate campanile with two clock faces. The mile-long avenue to the house from the main gates near Greenane is lined with rhododendrons.

The Glenmalure Barracks at Drumgoff, commenced in 1803, was smaller than those built at Glencree, Laragh and Aghavannagh. I have come across two near contemporary illustrations of the barracks, one by Petrie dated c.1820, an engraving in T.K. Cromwell's *Excursions through Ireland – Province of Leinster*, and another, from a very similar angle and almost the same viewpoint from the north-west, showing the same winding Military Road and the same profiles of Fananierin and Slieve Maan, by George Victor du Noyer, dated around 1840. What is interesting is the fact that Petrie's drawing is incorrect in its portrayal of the barracks itself: he shows wings at both ends of the long block, each a storey higher than the main block as at Glenmalure and Aghavannagh. It is as if he never visited Drumgoff and assumed the barracks here was the same as the others. Du Noyer's delicate drawing, however, is correct, including the eleven bays in the elevation, and showing no terminating wings. I wonder was he simply correcting the work of his old teacher, George Petrie?

The barracks built at Drumgoff and the business it promised, with a proposed garrison of one hundred men, attracted an Englishman called Wiseman to open an inn there in the early years of the 19th century. The expected custom from the soldiers was short-lived owing to the Battle of Waterloo, but it was more than replaced by the influx of miners and by the increase in tourists seeking scenic Wicklow in the peaceful early decades of the 19th century.

Anne Plumptre, who stayed at the Drumgoff Inn during her tour of Ireland in 1815, was not impressed, however, when kept waiting two hours for a chicken lunch. No inn could be opened without the approval of the local landlord, and in this case it is possible that Lord Meath, who had a residence at Ballincor to the east, would have found

Drumgoff Barracks c. 1840 by George Victor du Noyer
Courtesy of Royal Society of the Antiquaries of Ireland

uses for such a place close by, and may even have assisted financially. The following description by a traveller suggests such in 1826:

> We should not omit to observe that in the vicinity of the barracks is an inn, of a homely character, but well provided with the essentials of accommodation. As proof that a traveller visiting Glendaloch, or otherwise led to this remote tract, need not fear trusting the comforts of this 'hostel', it may be observed the present writer, in September, 1819, succeeded in the occupancy of the principal apartments to a noble earl and his lady, who possess much neighbouring property, and had passed several days on this recluse spot.[77]

The first edition *Wright's Guide to Wicklow*, the most successful guide to

---

77 Brewer, 1826.

the county of the 19th century, describes the place in 1822 as 'a most comfortable inn, kept by an English settler'. Many notable people stayed here, including the poet Thomas Moore, on his way south to Avoca in the 1820s, and a hundred years later, Evelyn Waugh spent nine days with a companion at Drumgoff in 1924, having left London with only £10 between them, and wrote:

> We had an awful fear on the first night that we had come to a Temperance Hotel; all the ashtrays and things advertised mineral waters and a pot of tea was brought to us at dinner. We found, however, that at great expense we could obtain a ghastly sort of ale, very fizzy and tasting strongly of baking powder, or a spirituous liquor – a mixture of bad rum, bad gin and bad vodka called whiskey, and, of course, the ubiquitous Bass. We walked a lot at Glenmalure and telegraphed for money a good deal which eventually arrived. The day I enjoyed most was when we walked to Glendalough and saw the seven churches and lay in St Kevin's Bed. On the whole I did not enjoy Glenmalure. One thing of profit happened. We buried my stick in a peat bog to see if it would colour it and it turned out quite black.

Waugh did for a time consider buying a property in Ireland, particularly after World War II, when very fine houses and estates could be bought for a song: Leonard Mosley, with whom he would have had connections through the Mitfords, bought a house in Galway in 1951, and Waugh wrote to Nancy Mitford in 1952:

> Among the countless blessings I thank God for my failure to find a house in Ireland comes first. Unless one is mad for fox hunting there is nothing to draw one. The houses, except for half a dozen famous ones, are very shoddy in building and they none of them have servants bedrooms because at the time they were built Irish servants slept on the kitchen floor. The peasants are malevolent. All their smiles are as false as Hell. Their priests are very suitable for them but not for foreigners. No coal at all. Awful incompetence everywhere. No native capable of doing the simplest job properly.

Wiseman ran the inn at Drumgoff until well into the 19th century, since which it has had a succession of owners, including for a time

Drumgoff Barracks today

Lord Meath, who fitted it out as a hunting lodge. At time of writing it is run by the Dowling family, who have been there since 1964, and during their time the place has been much extended and improved, and is rarely not booked out in summertime.

Signs of the mining past of Glenmalure are visible in many places in the valley, the most visible being what is called The Zig-Zags, a mine road that climbs steeply up the southern side of the valley near a fine waterfall. The Royal Irish Mining Company opened a number of adits in the early 19th century in search of galena, the ore that yields lead, which had been successfully mined in the next valley to the north, Glendalough. In those early years over three hundred tons of galena were extracted from Glenmalure: 86 percent of galena is lead, and on average, a ton of lead gave five ounces of silver, so the harvest from the mines here, if not as good as that from Glendalough or Glendasan, was reasonable. The military barracks at Drumgoff lost even its

Drumgoff Inn

skeleton garrison a few years after the end of the Napoleonic Wars, and it reverted to the Kemmis family, the original landowners. They sold the barracks in 1838 to the Royal Irish Mining Company, who used it as a hostel for their miners. By 1841, in addition to the barracks, twenty-six houses in the valley were occupied by miners.

If you venture west and deeper into Glenmalure, the flat bottom narrows to nothing and the valley becomes V-shaped: crossing the river by the ford at Barravore, the sides of the valley, increasing in steepness, seem to close in on the narrow road. Before Francis and Iseult Stuart moved into Laragh Castle, they spent the fractious early years of their marriage in an isolated two-storey cottage at the head of the glen that had been bought in 1919 by Maud Gonne McBride. Near it was the location chosen by J. M. Synge for his play *In the Shadow of the Glen*, in which a woman whose husband has died takes up a passing tramp's offer to come and travel the roads with him. In those days before the advent of radio and television, theatre was a very important medium of

Cottage at Barravore

communication, much subscribed to by the public, rich or poor, and often controversial. On the opening night of Synge's play in 1903, Maud Gonne walked out of the theatre as a protest 'against the intrusion of decadence'; the Irish theatre-going public were always hostile to what they felt was Synge's Anglo-Irish condescension, and four years later his play *The Playboy of the Western World* caused riots in Dublin.

Over the years many literary and political personages enjoyed the isolation of the little cottage at Barravore, including Countess Markievicz, Lennox Robinson, Dorothy McArdle, Rosamund Jacob, W.B. Yeats and Mrs Margaret Pearse. It was bequeathed in 1955 by the then owner, Dr Kathleen Lynn, on her death, to An Oige, the Irish Youth Hostel Association. It is still run by An Oige and must be one of their prettiest hostels. Nearby are a number of stone structures that date from the period when mining was carried on in the glen.

Leaving Drumgoff and Glenmalure, the Military Road climbs steadily again for some 5km to reach its final high pass at nearly 300m above sea level between Croaghanmoira and Slieve Maan, on an eastern spur of Lugnaquilla. There is a carpark at the pass, and an opportunity to savour the experience of standing on the summit of one of the highest mountains in Wicklow with the minimum of effort. The conical peak of Croaghanmoira, at 664m above sea level, is just over 1.5km (a mile) away to the east, with a gentle climb of 214m (700 feet) along a rough track. From this unparalleled vantage-point the views are superb.

Beyond the pass, a final winding descent finally brought the Military Road in 1809 to Aghavannagh where it connected with the pre-existing Hume's Road, built sometime after 1760 to connect Kiltegan in the west with Aughrim.

Aghavannagh is no more than a hamlet of a few houses, so insignificant that it is not even named on the Discovery Series Ordnance Maps. The big house on the right at the junction is said to have been a shop at one time, and there are those who stayed in the An Oige Youth Hostel who suggest that it was a sheebeen in the 1940s. It was run at the time by a woman with the unfortunate An Oige nickname of Hairy Essey, who is said to have sold alcohol from 'under the counter'.

The Military Road runs a short distance beyond the hamlet to connect with Hume's Road (linking Kiltegan and Aughrim), crossing the Aghavannagh and Ow rivers on the way, where the two bridges mentioned in Taylor's report of April 1806, costing £500 each, were required. The first, that over the Aghavannagh, with its gently curved parapets and circular buttresses with massive comma-shaped capstones each cut from a single slab of granite, went well beyond mere function, and looks like the final design for which the Drumgoff Bridge was the prototype. The bridge over the Ow was of similar design to that at Aghavannagh, but it had to be replaced in 1907 with what was at the time a unique ferro-concrete decked structure.[78] One of the last tasks to be carried out by Taylor's crew was the construction of an access road from the Military Road to the Aghavannagh barracks, which had been completed six years before.

---

78 *Alexander Taylor's Roadworks in Ireland 1780 to 1827*, Peter J. O'Keefe.

The barracks was built on an elevated gravel ridge between the two rivers, and over the last two hundred years has had almost as varied a series of uses as the barracks at Glencree. In spite of this, and the removal of one wing and the gutting of the other by fire, it is the least altered of the barracks and the central section is still in its original form.

Even the roof, although now deteriorating due to lack of maintenance since 1998, is substantially original, and the great double Bangor slates covering it are still secured by oak dowels. The original fresh water well can still be seen in the kitchen area, presumably put there rather than out in the grounds to prevent the water supply being poisoned by Michael Dwyer's men, and the gunpowder magazine, a thick walled store, is still in place.

After the building was vacated by the military about 1825, it reverted back to the ownership of the ground landlord, William Parnell of Avondale, who was fond of shooting and who occasionally used it as a 'shooting box'. Part of the barracks was occupied for some years in the 1840s by the newly founded Royal Irish Constabulary, which on occasions of local unrest apparently put in a garrison of up to fifty policemen. William's son, Charles Stewart Parnell, continued to use part of the building as a shooting box, and frequently brought parties there for a few days grouse-shooting on the hills around Aghavannagh. A spring on nearby Fearbreague Mountain is known by the locals as Parnell's Well, and a legend retailed by Parnell's old gamekeeper, Patrick O'Toole, told of a 2-mile long secret passage from the old barracks to a spot near the top of the mountain. A contemporary reference by a fellow MP suggests that Parnell himself often cooked dinner for his guests.

During his ownership, the building was renovated and made more comfortable, with some of the defensive half-circle arched windows on the ground floor being opened up. An engine was installed on the ground floor that turned coal into gas to provide heating and light: the engine is still there. Lawns and gardens were laid out in the grounds, and the avenue from the gate to the house was planted with trees. He loved the place and frequently walked there from his home at Avondale, 9 miles to the south. He became interested in the production of peat on Blackrock Hill, 2 miles to the west, which was considered to

One of the original defensive windows at Aghavannagh

be the best 'in the whole country', and pondered how production could economically assist his tenants in Aghavannagh. They, however, took advantage of his good nature and not only did not pay their rents, but almost denuded his Aghavannagh estate of game.

IN MEMORY OF THE CHIEF

Gathered from Aghavannagh's rugged side,
Where we together oft in friendship came,
Where Lugnacuilla rears its crest of pride,
And Glenmalure enshrines a Nation's fame,
Emblem of solitude, from his own hills, I lay this wreath
    where lies our glorious Chief,
To symbolize the solitude that fills
The Nation's lonely heart, that aches with endless grief.

W. J. CORBETT, 1892

When Parnell's premature death came on 6 October 1891, John Redmond succeeded him as leader of the Irish Party.

Aghavannagh Barracks

He had been loyal to Parnell through the difficult times, and got on well with him, partly no doubt because of their shared love of grouse-shooting and country life, and the fact that they were both 'gentlemen'. After Parnell's death the old barracks had to be disposed of, and some friends clubbed together to buy the place for Redmond, for 'his services to Ireland'.[79] The deeds cost a total of £250.

In Parnell's days the north and south wings of the building were in a ruinous condition, and the hunting lodge occupied the middle section. Although later commentaries suggest that Redmond largely rebuilt the place and turned it into 'a fine residence', during my visit to the building, derelict since 1998, the Spartan rooms could have been little different from the time when it was used as a barracks. It is likely that Parnell and Redmond transformed the place simply by decoration, carpets and furnishing. T.P. O'Connor, an MP during Redmond's time and an occasional visitor to Aghavannagh, wrote in his memoirs that the building

... stood on a hill, many miles from everybody and everything: it

79 *John Redmond* by Paul Bew, p.16, Dun Dealgan Press, 1996.

Fireplace in what
was John Redmond's
Library

consisted of a centre which was fairly comfortable, but on both sides there was a gaping wound where the wall stood bare and empty with no roof upon it.[80]

Like Parnell before him, Redmond used the building for gatherings of male chums for a weekend's shooting in the hills around. He kept what must have been a considerable part of his library there, which suggests that he spent long periods in residence, and clearly, it became as loved by him as it had been by Parnell. The library remained after his death, when the place passed to his son, William Redmond. When William died in 1932, the library was auctioned off, and one shudders to think of the fine collection of books dispersed for such a small income, as evidenced by the following note in the *Irish Book Lover*, September October 1932 edition:

---

80 *Memoirs of an Old Parliamentarian*, T.P. O'Connor London 1929.

The sale of the library of the late John Redmond at Aghavannagh was singularly disappointing; the prices realised being in many cases merely nominal, notwithstanding the fact that many of the volumes were presentation copies and bore autograph inscriptions. Whether it is the changed political outlook, the depressed condition of things in general, or the distant locality of the sale ... but the fact that a book like my old friend Grattan Flood's *History of Irish Music* with an inscription, went for a shilling, causes me furiously to think.

Later in the 1930s a Mrs G. E. Warwick was in residence, and when she moved to a smaller place in County Carlow, her companion, a Miss Mary Phelan, was left to look after Aghavannagh as caretaker. In 1939 Mrs Warwick loaned the building to An Oige and Miss Phelan undertook to stay on as hostel warden. She continued in that role after An Oige purchased the building for £350 in 1944, and became a much-loved and legendary character to hostel-goers over the next two decades. By the late 1940s Aghavannagh had become a very popular hostel: annual bed nights increased from 2,346 in 1946 to over 3,000 in 1948. With no electricity or running water conditions there were Spartan, but no one was ever turned away. The use of the hostel reached its peak in 1984 when there were over 5,400 bed nights, but the continuing deterioration of the building called for frequent voluntary work gangs to carry out repairs and maintenance. By 1998, however, at nearly two hundred years old, the building had deteriorated beyond what makeshift repairs could remedy, and it had to be closed. Efforts to attract sufficient funds to properly renovate the building to modern standards have so far failed.

The only visual vestiges remaining today of the occupation by Parnell and Redmond are probably the cast iron fireplaces on the first floor, but by whom they were installed is not clear. One of them in particular, of a classical design with ionic pilasters, can just about conjure up what the room and furnishings might have been like in the days of these two great parliamentarians.

Epilogue

While there is no doubt that the early years of the 19th century saw the end of the effectiveness of the Wicklow mountains as a place of safety for rebels and bandits on a large scale, I found no claims in the accounts and reports of the period that the Wicklow Military Road had played a major role in the matter. While there is one official report extant (*see page 157*) of damage to the value of one guinea being caused to the barracks at Leitrim in the Glen of Imaal while it was under construction, in spite of legends of Dwyer's delaying activities, there seems to have been no real concerted effort on the rebels' part to hinder or delay construction work. Furthermore, I found no reports of rebel interference with the construction of the Military Road itself over the nine years it took to complete. Indeed, it may be possible that parts of it were used as much, if on a smaller scale, by the rebels for fast communications and transport of weapons as it was used by the military. At best, the Wicklow Military Road and, perhaps more importantly, the barracks built along it, became a successful and powerful deterrent, a symbol of the potential of the English to wage total war.

While the overall route through the mountains planned by Alexander Taylor for the Military Road cannot be argued with, the reason he chose the route he did along the section from Rathfarnham to the Featherbeds remains unclear. Why did he plan a route that took in the Killakee demesne, involving a considerable amount of new road construction, instead of using the pre-existing road from Ballyboden via Woodtown to the southern end of Killakee? Having chosen the Killakee route, why was the Ballyboden via Woodtown road used anyway, and the section through the Killakee demesne not built until considerably later? These questions will probably never be completely answered, but one is inclined to believe that if there is no engineering or economic logic in the scheme, and there doesn't appear to be, the route must have been influenced by political or other considerations.

Although a number of the progress reports and cost estimates for the Wicklow Military Road prepared by Alexander Taylor are extant in contemporary documentation, to my layman's eye the figures given for distances and costs seem to vary between reports and are difficult to interpret accurately. In April 1802 Taylor states that the first 15 miles, including the bridges, cost £9,400, or £627 per mile, close enough to the figure mentioned in his letter of two months earlier, where he says: 'In July 1799 ... I mentioned the range of estimate of it at £500 the mile exclusive of bridges, sewers, and water pavements, and from the experience of what has been since done, I still think that sum will be sufficient, as no part of the intended road of a similar extent will more expensive than that now in hand.' He went on to say that there were no bridges of magnitude, but rather a great many small bridges and sewers etc. In the same report he estimates the cost of completion to Aghavannagh at a further £10,900, giving a total of £20,300, or £615 per Irish mile for what he reckons is 33 miles. By the time he prepared his progress report of April 1806, however, some escalation has occurred: the length of the road seems somehow to have increased to 34 Irish miles, and he estimates the final cost at £39,430 or £1,142 per Irish mile. By the actual completion three years later, the final cost had risen to about £43,500, or about £1,260 per Irish mile, which is considerably more than other contemporaneous roads through similar terrain. Richard Griffith's military roads through the Boggeragh Mountains of north-west Cork and across Keeper Hill in County Tipperary, built between 1822 and 1836, came out at an average of £785 per Irish mile.[81]

There were, of course, delays and periods when Dublin Castle was less anxious to have the project completed, as for instance when Michael Dwyer and his men gave themselves up in December 1803, all of which were bound to add to the cost. But for a few isolated cases of banditry, the large numbers of rebels who had held out in the mountains in the years

---

81   *Alexander Taylor's Roadworks in Ireland*, Peter O'Keefe, p. 100.

after the rebellion had all drifted away by 1804, and the only impetus remaining after that was the French threat. Taylor frequently lost much of his military manpower, and always had difficulty getting satisfactory local labour. During periods when the poad was not progressing he probably devoted much of his time to his private practice, so the Military Road may not have had his full attention in the later years, and it is likely that he left much of the work on site to his assistants. In a letter dated 25th April 1809 to Secretary Littlehales he apologises, saying he took immediate action to address Littlehales's requests as directed but was prevented, 'by ill health (Rhumatizm) from going to the County for some time after I received your letter, I have to apologise for not having been able to accomplish them sooner'. He was, after all, aged sixty-three at the time, and commuting between his office at Harcourt Road in Dublin and deepest Wicklow in all weathers would have required a good degree of fitness.

There is no doubt, however, that during the latter years of the building of the road, Alexander Taylor was a busy man, notwithstanding his 'rhumatizm'. He had been running a successful private practice since coming to Ireland, preparing maps of a high standard, such as the Map of the County of Kildare of 1783, and carrying out surveys such as that for the new harbour at Howth, and by the 1800s he had established a widely known reputation for professional competence and getting things done. Apart from his own road works, he had a financial involvement in other projects, such as County Kildare and County Limerick toll roads, in both of which he held shares. While his map-making business did not expand as he would have wished, after 1800, apart from the Map of the Environs of Dublin of 1805, he seems to have concentrated on road surveys, while one of his assistants, William Larkin, went on to considerable success by carrying out surveys and making maps of estates and a number of counties. Larkin was one of a number of Irish surveyors who owed their expertise in the use of modern surveying instruments, such as the theodolite, to Taylor, his brother George and their one-time partner Andrew Skinner.[82]

There were also other matters that demanded Alexander Taylor's attention. He was appointed Inspector of Designs and Surveys of Post

---

82 *Plantation Acres*, J. H. Andrews, p.356, United Historical Foundation, 1985.

Roads by the Post Office in 1805, and given the responsibility of having detailed surveys carried out of all the main post roads in Ireland. This involved employing a large number of surveying staff, and he took on his brother George to look after the Dublin to Kilkenny road, his former assistant William Larkin for the Dublin to Enniskillen route, and William Duncan for the Dublin to Wexford road. Taylor was in receipt of a salary of 500 guineas a year for this post.

The streets of Dublin were in poor condition at the turn of the 19th century, and in 1807 Alexander Taylor was appointed Chief Paving Commissioner for the city, and was charged with carrying out extensive improvements to Dublin's streets. He held the post, with a salary of 600 guineas, until 1826, when he had reached the age of eighty.

In 1818 after the Post Road Surveys had been completed, the Commission for Auditing Public Accounts set up an enquiry to look into the monies that had been paid out in relation to the survey work. The enquiry auditors only covered the period from 1812 to 1817, but even so, they discovered significant 'discrepancies' in the costs involved, particularly in the area of carrying out re-surveys, the provision of maps and the payment of travel expenses claimed on surveying work. All the payments made during the period had been approved and certified by Major Taylor, and the auditors found that the expenses claimed by some of the surveyors were considerably in excess of what would be regarded as reasonable. Although it was Taylor's responsibility to periodically inspect the ongoing survey works on site to ensure that the people he hired were actually carrying out the work properly and that the expenses they claimed were correct, there seems to be no record that he himself claimed travel expenses. Had his 'Rhumatizm' become worse, preventing him from carrying out any inspections (he was, after all, seventy-one years of age in 1817), or was he just too busy, depending totally on the abilities and honesty of the people he had hired? Of the £21,372-18s-7d paid out during the period between 1813 and 1817, the enquiry disallowed nearly half, £10,662-10s in all. The money had, however, not been repaid by the recipients by as late as 1826, when a further enquiry raised the matter with the Earl of Ross, the Postmaster General. Ross declared that as Taylor was still receiving a salary of 500 guineas per annum from the Post Office, and the discrepancy had been his fault, the government should make him pay for it. There is no record that they ever did.

In January 1826 a Commission of Enquiry was set up to look into the workings and performance of the Paving Board. During the enquiry Mr James Hendrick, the treasurer of the Paving Board, gave evidence to the extent that Alexander Taylor had made a habit over a period of ten years of drawing off advances of substantial sums of money, sometimes exceeding £800, from the Paving Board funds for his own personal use. When it was put to him, Taylor did not deny any of Hendrick's evidence. Perhaps more importantly, it was also found that records detailing how the £40,000 granted to the Paving Board had been spent were very scanty indeed.

All this has an amusingly contemporary ring to it. It is said that Taylor, described by the biographer of one of his descendants, General Sir Alexander Taylor,[83] as 'able, strong-headed, strong-tempered and adventurous', remained always a 'true Scot', and was not a popular man in Dublin. A newspaper of the time referred bitterly to him and his fellow Scotsmen engineers and surveyors, who were changing the shape of Ireland, as 'surly Taylor, the paver; slim Nimmo, the scurvy: or sly little Billy the Bald; knights of the chain and compass, or mere land surveyors, transported or imported here from Scotland'.[84] The Nimmo referred to was Alexander Nimmo, who designed many harbours and roads in the west of Ireland, and Bald was William Bald, described by J. H. Andrews as 'one of the half-dozen ablest, most hard working and most creative map-makers ever to practice in Ireland'. There is also no doubt but Taylor himself was an expert in his field, but one cannot help but wonder if he had more in mind than perfecting his art. As a young man in Scotland, Taylor had been accused of accepting a bribe from a Lieutenant Grant for altering a boundary line he was surveying. At the time, surveyors were seen as fair game to claims of inaccuracy and bribery, and Taylor strenuously denied the charge.[85]

---

83 Alicia Taylor, *General Sir Alex. Taylor 1826 to 1912*.
84 *A Letter to the Nobility, Gentry, and Landholders, of the County of Mayo, on the Waste or Misapplication of the County Cess, or Acre Money*, 1822, p.27.
85 *Alexander Taylor's Roadworks in Ireland 1780-1827* Peter O'Keefe, The Institute of Asphalt Technology, 1996

As a result of the Paving Board Enquiry of 1826, Alexander Taylor was removed from office. He retired from all his professional activities shortly after, and settled down in Naas, County Kildare, where he died, aged eighty-two, in 1828. He is buried in Maudlins Cemetery, Naas.

The Wicklow Military Road came into general use as each section was completed, although initially permission had to be obtained from the military authorities. The 'opening up' of the Wicklow wilderness as a result of the building of the road that was hoped for by some landowners failed to come about in any significant commercial sense, other than for access to hitherto inaccessible peat bogs and the transport of peat out of the mountains. In the 20th century the road enabled large areas of the mountains to be accessed for the planting of forests and for the extraction of timber. The experiment proposed in 1803 of creating a settlement of loyal peasantry in the high moors along the route failed to materialise, although for some years later the possibilities of draining and cultivating tracts of bog land in the mountains were still being discussed, and Taylor's success in drying out the route of the Military Road was often referred to. In 1813, Richard Griffith, in his Report on the Bogs of the Dublin and Wicklow Mountains, suggests that

> ...it is not too late to attempt their colonisation ... no year passes without our hearing of ships sailing for America, containing poor Highland families obliged to leave their own country for want of proper encouragement to remain. If part of these poor wanderers were induced to change their course, and settle in the Wicklow mountains, on Government granting to each family a small portion of land, we should soon behold a sturdy race of loyal mountaineers who would not only greatly improve the appearance of the country but would strengthen the hands of the Government by rendering what was lately considered the shelter for lawless rebels the residence of a population grateful to those who had rescued them from transatlantic emigration.

The transatlantic emigration of the Highlanders continued, however, to be followed within decades by an outflow from Ireland, and apart from the road, Mr Brady's house at Carrigshouk, and the 'Mountain House' at Cloghoge Brook, much of the high moorland through which the Military Road passes remains untouched by the hand of man.

The tourism potential of the Military Road was spotted early. Only a year after work started, the road was praised by Robert Fraser in his *Statistical Survey of County Wicklow* of 1801 and he went on to say:

> By means of this road there will not only be an easy and ready access for the army, to preserve the peace and quite of adjacent districts, but there will be an opening to Enterprise and Capital to speculate in cultivating these at present uninhabited wilds, and to ornament the many beautiful lakes and valleys, which abound in the midst of this extensive region.
>
> Beautiful rides will also be formed to the adjacent summits, from many of which an extensive prospect is commanded of the beautiful vales of the county Wicklow to the east, and the expanse of St George's Channel, and a distant view of the mountains of Wales.

The first edition of what was to become a very successful travellers guide, G. N. Wright's *Tours in Ireland*, makes full use of the Military Road in 1822, which it calls 'the little Irish Simplon'. With regard to Lough Bray it makes the following comments:

> ...the convenient distance of Lough Bray from Dublin (ten miles) affords the citizens an opportunity of amusing themselves along its shores, and after enjoying a cold collation, returning to town in the evening. There is a great abundance of trout in both the upper and lower lakes, both bog and grey trout, principally the former, but the want of a boat is a great preventative to successful angling; the only method that is likely to succeed without one, is cross-fishing by two persons.

The Grand Jury took over the maintenance of the road in 1842, but it remained little more than a mountain track for another hundred years. Early in World War II, however, when coal supplies began to run out in Ireland, the government set up the Turf Development Board. County Councils were empowered to take over bogs in their area and harvest the peat for fuel. Dublin had the biggest fuel shortage problem and needed

10,000 tons of turf per week to keep going. To redress this situation, new bogs were opened in County Kildare from where peat could be shipped by canal to the city, and the Military Road into Wicklow was strengthened and surfaced from the Featherbeds to the Sally Gap so that it could take lorries heavily loaded with turf. Nationally, over one million tons of peat were saved during 1941, and the surplus was stockpiled in high stacks in the Phoenix Park. Thousands of individual Dubliners also leased plots in the Featherbed/Glencree area to harvest their own peat, starting a family tradition that lasted well into the 1970s.

When Ireland began to find its economic feet in the 1960s, the County Dublin section of the Military Road below the Featherbeds began to attract residential development. Although the number of residents of Glencree engaged in farming activities has been steadily decreasing for decades, there has been an increase in the building of individual houses there over the past ten years. Glenmacnass has similarly seen an increase in single dwellings along the floor of the valley but from the Featherbeds to Glenmacnass and from south of Laragh to Aghavannagh the landscape through which the Military Road passes has lost little of its character as a true wilderness. There is no doubt, however, that this wilderness is becoming more vulnerable in the current period of prosperity in Ireland.

In this increasingly urbanised world, the existence of and access to wilderness areas are now generally accepted as being fundamentally important to the health of society. Ireland's low population and relatively late industrial revolution has ensured that we have not yet eaten up all our open spaces, and the conservation of what is left should be of the utmost importance. Gerard Manley Hopkins put it succinctly nearly a century and a half ago:

> What would the world be, once bereft
> Of wet and of wildness? Let them be left,
> O let them be left, wildness and wet;
> Long live the weeds and the wilderness yet.

There are increasing signs that the edges of the Wicklow upland wilderness are under threat. With the continuing suburbanisation policies of the planners with regard to the population of the capital, the northern fringes of the uplands above Killakee and the valley of Glencree are particularly vulnerable: a significant area of the Featherbeds, where people have walked over heather for many years, is in private hands, and signs threatening to prosecute trespassers are springing up. It is clear that a particularly concentrated effort is needed by the Wicklow and Dublin local authorities to harden up their planning policies if we are not to lose what precious wilderness we have remaining to us in the area.

In spite of its high population relative to Ireland, the nature of land ownership in Britain and the enactment over the last century and more of visionary legislation have allowed large areas of rural land close to cities to be protected from development and made available for the amenity and recreation of its urban people. If Ireland had the same population as Britain per square mile, we would have to share our space with thirty-four million people: while this level is not likely in the near future, our population is rising dramatically, and new and imaginative thinking is needed now to plan for the conservation of our countryside and the use of it for recreation in parallel, where appropriate, with agriculture.

The protection of areas like the Wicklow uplands needs radical measures: the Military Road can be seen as both a useful amenity and a threat. Care needs to be taken to resist 'improving' it too much, and thought must be given to some element of restriction of the amount and type of traffic that uses it. Indeed, I do not think it is unreasonable to suggest that, apart from measures to conserve the existing Wicklow landscape and secure the facility of its use for recreational purposes, a significant contribution might be to close the stretch of the Military Road from the Sally Gap to Glenmacnass to all but local vehicular use. This would create 170 sq km of wild landscape that would be a magnificent amenity close to our capital city.

Even as it stands, the Military Road is an ideal access route to 750 sq km of Irish upland, and should remain so if local authorities restrict inappropriate development and are not tempted to 'improve' it any further. Built for war-like purposes, the Wicklow Military Road today provides people from home and abroad with amenity, pleasure and peace.

Bibliography

Andrews, J.H., *Plantation Acres*, Ulster Historical Foundation,1985

Archer, Joseph, *Statistical Survey of County Dublin*, Dublin, 1801

Ball, F. E. *A History of the County Dublin*, The HSP Library, 1995

Beckett, J. C., *The Making of Modern Ireland 1603-1923*, Faber, 1971

Bew, Paul, *John Redmond*, Dundalgan Press, 1996

Brewer, J. N. *The Beauties of Ireland*, London, 1826

Costello, Peter, *James Joyce: The Years of Growth 1882 – 1915*, Pantheon, 1993

Cromwell, Thomas, *Excursions Through Ireland*, London 1820

Dickson, Charles, *The Life of Michael Dwyer*, Browne and Nolan, 1944

Donnelly, N., *A Short History of Dublin Parishes*, Carraig Chapbooks

Dublin Penny Journal, Various

Dublin Historical Record, Various

Elborn, Geoffrey, *Francis Stuart – A Life*, Raven Arts Press 1990

Feehan & O'Donovan, *The Bogs of Ireland*, University College Dublin, 1996

Ferran, Paddy, *Notes on Aghavannagh*, private

Fewer, Michael, *A Walk in Ireland*, Atrium, 2002

Fitton, William: *Notice respecting the geological structure in the vicinity of Dublin*, *Transactions of the Geological Society of London*, 1811

Foster, Roy, *Modern Ireland, 1600-1972*, Viking, 1989

Fraser, Robert, *General View of the Agriculture and Minerology of County Wicklow*, Dublin 1801

Freeman's Journal Various

Gardeners Chronicle, 1864

Guedella, Philip, *The Duke*, Wordsworth Editions, 1997

Hannigan & Nolan ed. *Wicklow History and Society*, Geography Productions, 1994

Healy, Patrick, *Rathfarnham Roads*, South Dublin Libraries, 2005

Hoare, Richard, *Journal of a Tour in Ireland AD 1806*, London 1807

Igoe, Vivian, *Dublin Burial Grounds and Graveyards*, Wolfhound, 2001

Jeffares, A. Norman, *W. B. Yeats*, Hutchinson, 1988

Journal of the Royal Society of the Antiquaries of Ireland, Various

Joyce, Weston St John, *The Neighbourhood of Dublin*, Gill, 1921

Lamb & Bowe, *A History of Gardening in Ireland*, National Gardens, 1995

Lewis's Topographical Dictionary

Luckholme, Philip, *A Tour Through Ireland*

Malton's Dublin 1799, Dolmen Press

Manning, Conleth, *Wicklow Archaeology and History*, Volume 1, County Wicklow Archaeological Society, 1998

Maxwell, Constantia, *Dublin under the Georges, 1714 –1830* , George Harrap, 1936

Martin, John, *An Illustrated Survey of An Oige's Youth Hostels*, Nonsuch Press 2006

Molohan, Cathy, *Germany and Ireland 1945-1955*, Irish Academic Press, 1999

O'Connell, Kevin J, *A Brief History of Television in Ireland*, 1998.

O'Donnell, Ruane, *Exploring Wicklow's Rebel Past 1798-1803*, Wicklow '98 Committee, 1998

O'Donnell, Ruan, *The Rebellion in Wicklow 1798*, O.D.C., 1998

O'Keefe, Peter J, *Alexander Taylor's roadways in Ireland, 1780 – 1827*, Institute of Asphalt Technology, 1995

Oman, Carola, *Britain Against Napoleon*, Faber and Faber, 1942

Pakenham, Thomas, *The Year of Liberty*, Hodder & Stoughton, 1969

Parnell, J. H., *Charles Stewart Parnell*, Cassell, 1973

Power, Pat, *The County Wicklow Military Road – A History*, private, 2000

by Price, Liam, *Placenames of Wicklow*, Dublin Institute of Advanced Studies, 1967

Pyatt, Edward, *Mountains of Britain*, Batsford, 1966

Rutty, John, An Essay towards the Natural History of County Dublin, Dublin 1757

Sleator, Matthew, Topography and Itinerary of Counties of Ireland, Dublin 1806

Stuart, Madelaine, *Manna in the Morning*, Raven Arts Press, 1984

Sullivan, Dennis, *A Picturesque Tour Through Ireland 1824*, London, 1825

Taylor and Skinner, *Maps of the Roads of Ireland*, Irish University Press, 1969

Taylor, Alicia, *Sir Alexander Taylor 1826-1912*

The Post Chaise Companion or Travellers Directory Through Ireland, Dublin 1802

Tracy, Frank, *If Those Trees Could Speak*, South Dublin Libraries, 2005

Walker's Hibernian Magazine, November 1803

Wickwire, F&M, *Cornwallis, the Imperial Years*, University of N Carolina, 1980

Index

Page numbers underlined refer to maps or illustrations; those in italics refer to chapters; 'n' following a page number refers to a footnote; (mt) indicates a mountain.